Caroline Lavinia Scott Harrison

Statesmen's Dishes and how to Cook them.

Caroline Lavinia Scott Harrison
Statesmen's Dishes and how to Cook them.
ISBN/EAN: 9783744789509

Printed in Europe, USA, Canada, Australia, Japan

Cover: Foto ©Lupo / pixelio.de

More available books at **www.hansebooks.com**

STATESMEN'S DISHES;

AND

HOW TO COOK THEM.

PRACTICAL AUTOGRAPHIC RECIPES

BY

Mrs. BENJAMIN HARRISON,

Mrs. WILLIAM WINDOM,   Mrs. D. J. BREWER,
Mrs. JOHN WANAMAKER,   Mrs. JOHN J. INGALLS,
Mrs. WILLIAM H. H. MILLER,   Mrs. JOHN SHERMAN,
Mrs. JOHN W. NOBLE,   Mrs. JOHN H. REAGAN,
Mrs. JERE. M. RUSK,   Mrs. M. S. QUAY,
Mrs. MELVILLE W. FULLER,   Mrs. M. C. BUTLER,
Mrs. SAMUEL F. MILLER,   Mrs. T. B. REED,
Mrs. STEPHEN J. FIELD,   Mrs. JOHN G. CARLISLE,

AND

Mrs. MORRISON R. WAITE,

Mrs. JOHN A. LOGAN,   Mrs. PHILIP H. SHERIDAN,

AND MORE THAN TWO HUNDRED OTHER WOMEN PROMINENT
IN OFFICIAL AND SOCIAL LIFE AT THE
NATIONAL CAPITAL.

WASHINGTON, D. C.
THE NATIONAL TRIBUNE.
MDCCCXC.

BRENTANO'S,
NEW YORK,
CHICAGO, WASHINGTON, PARIS, LONDON.

PREFACE.

WASHINGTON, our beautiful National Capital, is famous for many things, but in nothing has it so pleasing a reputation as for refined hospitality. In this charming respect no other city in the world surpasses it—indeed, it is believed that few, if any, equal it. Natural causes produce this. It is the political capital of many more millions of enlightened, progressive and wealthy people than are found in compact territory under any other flag in the world. Public business, the fluctuations of politics, ease of communication, and other reasons combine to bring, at one time or another, representatives at the best of all of these together in Washington. They meet under circumstances well calculated to promote the development of pleasant social intercourse. With them meet representatives of the most refined and cultivated society of the old world.

The result is that the art of entertaining is carefully cultivated, and all that is pleasant and graceful in the science of the table—which must always play so important a part in hospitality—receives its highest development.

This collection of practical recipes is of unprecedented interest and value. Nothing approaching it has ever before been offered the public. All the ladies who have kindly contributed are noted in Washington circles, and far beyond those confines, as hostesses and housekeepers. They are universally recognized as leaders, and the excellence of their entertainments has done very much toward building up the reputation of the Capital for refined hospitality.

The recipes given are for dishes which have received the enthusiastic commendation of the most critical diners-out. Most of them are specialties upon which the ladies pride themselves, and not a few are the inventions—the "creations" a French *chef de cuisine* would say—of the fair contributors.

We are tempted to expatiate at length upon many of these—to relate of some that they are cherished heirlooms, which have been in the families for generations, and handed down from mother to daughter; of others that they were conceived and elaborated years ago by young wives, anxious to excel in attractive tables, and retained by them because they accomplished their design. But to give these their proper history would make this book many times its present size; so we must refrain.

Trial will demonstrate more fully than any words can state the unusual value of these recipes.

WASHINGTON, D. C., *May*, 1890.

CONTENTS.

SOUPS.

		PAGE.
Clear Soup	Mrs. BENJAMIN HARRISON	15
Gumbo	Mrs. JOHN G. CARLISLE	16
Corn Soup	Mrs. ROSWELL P. FLOWER	17
Tomato Soup	Mrs. JULIUS C. BURROWS	18
Amber Soup	Mrs. JOHN H. ROGERS	19
Mock Turtle	Mrs. H. C. McCORMICK	20
A Quickly Made Soup	Mrs. HARRIET TAYLOR UPTON	21

FISH, OYSTERS, ETC.

Fish Chowder	Mrs. BENJAMIN HARRISON	22
Codfish Balls	Mrs. MELVILLE W. FULLER	23
Fish a la Lucullus	Mrs. JOHN W. NOBLE	24
Fish Chowder	Mrs. JOHN SHERMAN	25
Deviled Crabs	Mrs. M. S. QUAY	26
Broiled Oysters on Toast	Mrs. C. K. DAVIS	27
Baked Fish	Mrs. JAMES E. CAMPBELL	28
Stewed Oysters	Mrs. ROSWELL P. FLOWER	29
Baked Shad	Mrs. R. M. LA FOLLETTE	30
Scalloped Oysters	Mrs. J. R. McKEE	31
Codfish Fake	Col. GILBERT A. PIERCE	32
Terrapin	Hon. THOMAS F. BAYARD	33
Fish Chowder	Capt. G. E. THORNTON	34

CONTENTS.

ROASTS.

		PAGE.
Christmas Turkey	Mrs. STEPHEN J. FIELD	35
Baked Chicken	Mrs. THOMAS B. REED	36
Young Roast Pig	Mrs. J. N. CLARKSON	37
Saddle of Mutton	Mrs. J. LOWRIE BELL	39
Barbecued Mutton	Mrs. ROGER Q. MILLS	40
Roast Turkey	Mrs. THOMAS J. HENDERSON	41
Roast Beef	Mrs. W. D. BYNUM	42
Roast Veal	Mrs. A. C. HARMER	43
Baked Ham	Mrs. GEORGE T. BARNES	44
Roast Turkey	Mrs. GEORGE W. SMITH	45
Stuffed Ham	Mrs. THOMAS C. CATCHINGS	46

GAME.

Roast Duck	Mrs. JOHN J. INGALLS	47
Ortolans	Mrs. JAMES E. CAMPBELL	48

BREAD, ETC.

Canned Corn Patties	Mrs. WILLIAM WINDOM	49
Steam Brown Bread	Mrs. W. H. H. MILLER	50
Graham Gems	Mrs. W. H. H. MILLER	51
Bread	Mrs. JAMES F. WILSON	52
Corn Pone	Mrs. JAMES K. JONES	53
Corn Muffins	Mrs. CHARLES F. MANDERSON	54
Egg Bread	Mrs. WILLIAM B. BATE	55
Swedish Timbales	Mrs. J. S. C. BLACKBURN	56
Breakfast Cakes	Mrs. JOHN C. SPOONER	57
Milk Bread	Mrs. NELSON DINGLEY, JR	58
Beaten Biscuit	Mrs. JAMES H. BLOUNT	59
Salt-Rising Bread	Mrs. THOMAS R. STOCKDALE	60

CONTENTS.

PAGE.

Johnny Cakes	Mrs. W. O. ARNOLD	61
Sweet Corn Bread	Mrs. ALBERT C. THOMPSON	62
Common Biscuit	Mrs. ASHER G. CARUTH	63
Green Corn Fritters	Mrs. WILLIAM J. CONNELL	64
Fried Cakes	Mrs. GEORGE H. BRICKNER	65
Waffles	Mrs. ALBERT C. THOMPSON	66
Loaf Bread	Mrs. DANIEL M. RANSDELL	67
Cream Toast	Miss L. S. SWAN	68

ENTREES, OMELETS, ENTREMETS, ETC.

Sausage Rolls	Mrs. BENJAMIN HARRISON	69
Lemon Omelet	Mrs. M. S. QUAY	71
Mississippi Baked Hash	Mrs. JAMES Z. GEORGE	72
Beef Collar	Mrs. JAMES Z. GEORGE	73
Relish for Lunch	Mrs. THOMAS B. REED	74
Sweetbreads and Mushrooms	Mrs. J. N. HUSTON	75
Chicken Croquets	Mrs. A. W. GREELY	76
Pressed Chicken	Mrs. THOMAS J. HENDERSON	77
Veal Loaf	Mrs. J. G. SAWYER	78
Curried Mutton Chops	Mrs. JOSEPH E. WASHINGTON	79
Veal Fricandeau	Mrs. A. T. BLISS	80
Cream Chicken	Mrs. MARK S. BREWER	81
Plain Omelet	Mrs. WILLIAM E. MASON	82
Meat Soufflé	Mrs. ORREN C. MOORE	83
Veal Loaf	Mrs. JOHN A. PICKLER	84
Baked Omelet	Mrs. GEORGE H. BRICKNER	85
Puff Omelet	Mrs. W. E. SIMONDS	86
Boiling Eggs	Mrs. E. V. BROOKSHIRE	87
Chicken Croquets	Mrs. H. C. MCCORMICK	88
Boned Chicken	Miss JULIA DARLING STRONG	89
Chipped Beef	Miss L. S. SWAN	90
Deviled Eggs	Miss L. S. SWAN	91

CONTENTS.

VEGETABLES.

		PAGE.
Broiled Tomatoes	Mrs. N. P. BANKS	92
Mashed Potatoes	Mrs. R. P. BLAND	93
Minced Cabbage	Mrs. ROSWELL P. FLOWER	94
Cauliflower	Mrs. W. O. ARNOLD	95
Spinach	Mrs. JOHN M. FARQUHAR	96
Lima Beans	Mrs. MOSES D. STIVERS	97
Scalloped Sweet Potatoes	Mrs. WILLIAM J. CONNELL	98
Baked Potatoes	Mrs. JOSEPH McKENNA	99
Asparagus	Mrs. BENJAMIN F. SHIVELY	100
Green Peas	Mrs. J. R. WILLIAMS	101
Macaroni	Mrs. E. C. VENABLE	102
Egg Plant	Mrs. LEWIS F. WATSON	103
Green Vegetables	Mrs. S. A. CRAIG	104
Stewed Corn	Miss PHŒBE W. COUZINS	105

SALADS.

Chicken Salad	Mrs. STANLEY MATTHEWS	106
Lobster Salad	Mrs. JOHN WANAMAKER	107
Tomato Salad	Mrs. E. H. CONGER	108
Potato Salad	Mrs. S. A. CRAIG	109
Cold Slaw	Mrs. JASON B. BROWN	110
Crab Salad	Mrs. J. R. McKEE	111

SAUCES, RELISHES, ETC.

Chicken Sauce	Mrs. JOHN W. NOBLE	112
Chow Chow	Mrs. JOHN SHERMAN	216
Relish for Cold Meats	Mrs. M. S. QUAY	113
Chestnut Stuffing	Mrs. F. M. COCKRELL	114
Chicken Filling	Mrs. J. S. C. BLACKBURN	115

CONTENTS.

PAGE.

Catsup	Mrs. JOHN H. REAGAN	116
Picolli	Mrs. HENRY W. BLAIR	117
Mushroom Sauce	Mrs. C. A. BERGEN	118
Strawberry Sauce	Mrs. W. D. OWEN	119
Peach Sauce	Mrs. CHARLES C. TOWNSEND	120
Chicken Salad Dressing	Mrs. H. C. MCCORMICK	121
Central American Sirup	Mrs. R. M. LA FOLLETTE	122
Pudding Sauce	Mrs. JOHN B. HENDERSON	155

PUNCH, EGG-NOGG, ETC.

Maryland Egg-Nogg	Mrs. STEPHEN J. FIELD	123
Regent Punch	Mrs. JOHN E. KENNA	124
Milk Punch	Mrs. ROSWELL P. FLOWER	125
Apple Toddy	Mrs. JOS. E. WASHINGTON	126
Cider Nogg	Mrs. F. W. WHEELER	127
Unfermented Grape Juice	Mrs. ZERELDA C. WALLACE	128
Cabinet Punch	Mrs. JAS. B. RICKETTS	129

PUDDINGS, PIES, JELLIES, ETC.

Fig Pudding	Mrs. BENJAMIN HARRISON	130
Mince Pie	Mrs. SAMUEL F. MILLER	131
Graham Pudding	Mrs. W. H. H. MILLER	132
Jelly	Mrs. JERE M. RUSK	133
Temperance Punch	Mrs. W. H. H. MILLER	134
Russian Cream	Mrs. JERE M. RUSK	135
Fruit Pudding	Mrs. PHILIP H. SHERIDAN	136
Citron Pudding	Mrs. JOHN A. LOGAN	138
Meringue Pudding	Mrs. M. C. BUTLER	139
New England Indian Pudding	Mrs. HENRY W. BLAIR	140
Snow Pudding	Mrs. JAMES L. PUGH	141

CONTENTS.

		PAGE.
Lottie's Pudding	Mrs. WILLIAM P. HEPBURN	142
Russian Cream	Mrs. WILLIAM S. HOLMAN	143
Cream Pies	Mrs. C. A. BOUTELLE	144
Boiled Custard	Mrs. BYRON M. CUTCHEON	145
Plum Pudding	Mrs. ELLIOTT B. COUES	146
Charlotte Russe	Mrs. ISAAC S. STRUBLE	147
Cardinal Richelieu Pudding	Mrs. CHARLES H. GIBSON	148
Wolf Pudding	Mrs. R. H. NORTON	149
Tapioca Custard Pudding	Mrs. A. M. DOCKERY	150
Charlotte Russe	Mrs. CHARLES S. BAKER	151
Sponge Pudding	Mrs. WILLIAM E. MASON	152
Baked Custards	Mrs. A. C. HARMER	153
Charlotte Russe	Mrs. ALONZO NUTE	154
Pudding Sauce	Mrs. JOHN B. HENDERSON	155
Apple Pan Dowdy	Mrs. MARCUS A. SMITH	156
Boiled Pears	Mrs. WILLIAM H. MORROW	157
Apple Tapioca	Mrs. J. H. BANKHEAD	158
Plum Pudding	Mrs. JOSEPH E. MCDONALD	159
Cider Jelly	Mrs. D. J. BREWER	160
Dixie Pudding	Mrs. W. H. F. LEE	161
Bread Toté	Mrs. JOHN LIND	162
Pumpkin Pie	Mrs. J. W. VAN SCHAICK	163
Pie Crust	Mrs. J. W. VAN SCHAICK	164
Spanish Cream	Mrs. C. W. SPOFFORD	165

CAKES.

Old-fashioned Sponge Cake	Mrs. MORRISON R. WAITE	166
German Almond Rings	Mrs. WILLIAM WINDOM	167
Shakspere Cake	Mrs. WILLIAM WINDOM	168
Angel Food	Mrs. JERE M. RUSK	169
Harrison Fruit Cake	Mrs. JOHN J. INGALLS	170
Delicate Cake	Mrs. JOHN SHERMAN	171

CONTENTS.

		PAGE.
Berwick Sponge Cake	Mrs. WILLIAM P. FRYE	172
Gingerbread	Mrs. WILLIAM P. FRYE	173
Sponge Cake	Mrs. JOHN H. REAGAN	174
Sponge Cake	Mrs. GILBERT A. PIERCE	175
Sunshine Cake	Mrs. GIDEON C. MOODY	176
Mrs. Carlisle's Cake	Mrs. JOHN G. CARLISLE	177
What-is-Left-Over Cake	Mrs. JOHN H. GEAR	178
Breakfast Cake	Mrs. NELSON DINGLEY, JR	179
Spice Cake	Mrs. C. A. BOUTELLE	180
Strawberry Shortcake	Mrs. JOHN M. FARQUHAR	181
Caramel Cake	Mrs. W. D. BYNUM	182
Sponge Cake	Mrs. LEWIS E. PAYSON	183
Minnehaha Cake	Mrs. WILLIAM P. HEPBURN	184
Gold and Silver Cakes	Mrs. S. R. PETERS	185
English Walnut Cake	Mrs. W. H. GEST	186
Sponge Cake	Mrs. JOSEPH MCKENNA	187
Grandmother's Cake	Mrs. CHARLES A. RUSSELL	188
Snow Cake	Mrs. M. H. MCCORD	189
Fruit Cake	Mrs. R. A. PIERCE	190
Chocolate Caramel Cake	Mrs. J. W. FOSTER	191
Cocoanut Cake	Mrs. R. H. NORTON	192
Delicate Cake	Mrs. H. C. MCCORMICK	193
Ice Cream Cake	Mrs. R. F. PETTIGREW	194
Drop Cake	Mrs. ALONZO NUTE	195
Saucissons de Chocolat	Miss BESSIE SNIDER	196
Pecan Cake	Mrs. J. R. MCKEE	197
Pound Cake	Miss MARY E. TURPIE	198
Sponge Cake	Mrs. ISABELLA BEECHER HOOKER	199
Fruit Cake	Miss MARY E. TURPIE	200
Angel Food	Miss MARY E. TURPIE	201
Boiled Frosting	Miss MARY E. TURPIE	202
Chocolate Cream Cake	Miss LILLAH BRICKNER	203
Wedding Cake	Mrs. Gen. F. W. LANDER	218

CONTENTS

ICE CREAM, BONBONS, Etc.

		PAGE.
Bonbons	Mrs. SHELBY M. CULLOM	204
Chocolate Creams	Mrs. SHELBY M. CULLOM	205
Candied Sweet Potatoes	Mrs. M. C. BUTLER	206
Frozen Apricots	Mrs. M. S. QUAY	207
Oranges Filled with Jelly	Mrs. J. N. HUSTON	208
Crystallized Fruit	Mrs. CHARLES E. HOOKER	209
Ice Cream Without Eggs	Mrs. WILLIAM VANDEVER	210
Caramel Ice Cream	Mrs. H. C. HANSBROUGH	211
Orange Preserves	Mrs. CHARLES TRACEY	212
Deviled Almonds	Mrs. W. D. OWEN	213
Salted Almonds	Mrs. JOHN F. LACEY	214
Orange Fool	Mrs. DANIEL M. RANSDELL	215

MISCELLANEOUS.

President Harrison's Christmas Dinner	Mrs. BENJAMIN HARRISON	217
A Pink Dinner in Apartments	Mrs. WM. M. STEWART	219
A Good Baking Powder	Mrs. MARY A. DENISON	220
Healing Plaster	Mrs. ROSWELL P. FLOWER	221
To Clean Kid Gloves	Mrs. C. K. DAVIS	222

STATESMEN'S DISHES.

CLEAR SOUP.
BY MRS. BENJAMIN HARRISON.
(Wife of the President.)

**EXECUTIVE MANSION,
WASHINGTON.**

4 lbs of juicy beef
1 knuckle of veal
2 small turnips
2 "   carrots
1 soup bunch
1 small pod of red pepper
2 "   white onions
Salt
6 quarts of water
Boil six hours, then strain through a sieve — let stand one night & congeal — then skim off all the grease, put into a kettle to warm & add sherry or madeira wine to taste.
Caroline Scott Harrison.

GUMBO.

BY MRS. JOHN G. CARLISLE.
(Wife of Representative from Kentucky and ex-Speaker.)

ONE large chicken, cut in pieces and fried; put on in a gallon of water; fry three onions, two slices of breakfast bacon, and add with the chicken. Let boil two and a half hours; cut small one quart okra; stew one quart of tomatoes, season and add. Let boil one hour, add a little sugar and thicken with browned flour.

Mrs. J. G. Carlisle.

CORN SOUP.

BY MRS. ROSWELL P. FLOWER.
(Wife of Representative from New York.)

ONE pint of grated green corn, one quart of milk, one pint of hot water, one heaping tablespoonful of flour, two tablespoonfuls of butter, one sliced onion, salt and pepper to taste. Cook the corn in the water thirty minutes. Let the milk and onion come to a boil, have the flour and butter mixed together, then add a few tablespoonfuls of boiling milk. When perfectly smooth, stir into the milk and cook eight minutes; take out the onion and the corn; season to taste.

Sarah M. Flower

TOMATO SOUP.

BY MRS J. C. BURROWS.
(Wife of Representative from Michigan.)

ONE quart of stock, one quart of canned tomatoes, one onion, three sprigs of parsley, two cloves, one teaspoonful of butter, salt and pepper to taste. Boil half an hour; strain through a sieve; dissolve four tablespoonfuls of flour or cornstarch in cold water; stir in soup; boil five minutes. Serve with croutons.

Very Sincerely Yours
Frances P. Burrows.

AMBER SOUP.

BY MRS. JOHN H. ROGERS.
(Wife of Representative from Arkansas.)

ONE large soup-bone, one chicken, a small slice of ham, a soup bunch, one onion, two sprigs of parsley, one-half carrot, one-half parsnip, celery, three cloves, pepper, salt, one gallon of cold water, whites and shells of two eggs, and caramel for coloring. Boil beef, chicken and ham for five hours. The last hour add vegetables and cloves. Strain in an earthen bowl and let it remain over night. Next day remove the cake of fat on top, pour off the liquor, avoiding the settling. Mix into it the beaten whites of the eggs and shells. Boil quickly half a minute, and pass through a jelly-bag. Add a spoonful or two (enough to color) of caramel and two of pearl tapioca. This is especially nice for receptions, teas, etc., if served very hot.

TO MAKE THE CARAMEL.

Put in a saucepan a small quantity of brown sugar with a little water. Stir it constantly over the fire until it is a dark color. Be careful not to burn.

Mary D. Rogers

MOCK-TURTLE SOUP.

BY MRS. H. C. M'CORMICK.
(Wife of Representative from Pennsylvania.)

TAKE a scalded calf's head; boil it in hot water for twenty minutes; drain and put in cold water. Then place in a saucepan with three quarts of water, a carrot, an onion, four cloves, three cloves of garlic, a few branches of parsley, a tablespoonful of vinegar and a little salt. Mix well three tablespoonfuls of flour in a little water, which add to the other ingredients and boil gently for half an hour; drain, and when cold cut the calf's head into small pieces; then add about a quart of heavy stock, boil gently twenty minutes, and just before serving also add a good glass of sherry, a little red pepper and two hard-boiled eggs chopped up, the yolks and whites separately, and the peel of a lemon cut in small pieces.

*Ida H. McCormick
Williamsport,
Pa.*

A QUICKLY-MADE SOUP.

BY MRS. HARRIET TAYLOR UPTON.
(Daughter of Hon. E. B. Taylor, of Ohio, and author of "The Children c the White House.")

NOTHING perhaps is of more help to a house keeper than to be able to concoct at short notice a good soup. A meager lunch, or a light dinner is often turned into an attractive meal by the addition of a soup. Below is given one of the most simple of quickly-made soups:

Place one tablespoonful of butter in a stewpan till it boils but does not brown. Add two tablespoonfuls of flour; when all is thoroughly mixed add one teaspoonful of salt, one teaspoonful of celery salt, one saltspoonful of white pepper. Boil one quart of milk, and add the hot thickening. Remove the bone and skin from one small can of salmon; mince or chip it; add the fish to the milk, which, when once boiled, serve immediately.

Harriet T Upton

FISH CHOWDER.

BY MRS. BENJAMIN HARRISON.
(Wife of the President.)

CUT a medium-sized shad or white-fish, three or four potatoes, one onion and a quarter of a pound of bacon into small pieces. Fry the bacon and onions a light brown. Put a layer of potatoes in the saucepan, over that a layer of the fish, then a sprinkling of onions and bacon, then a layer of tomatoes; sprinkle with pepper and salt, alternating the layers until all is in. Add enough water to cover, place over a moderate fire and let simmer twenty-five minutes. Boil one pint of milk, thickening it with cracker crumbs; let it stand a moment and then add to the chowder. Now stir for the first time, let boil an instant, season if not strong to taste, and serve hot.

Caroline S. Harrison

CODFISH BALLS.

BY MRS. MELVILLE W. FULLER.
(Wife of the Chief Justice of the Supreme Court.)

EQUAL parts codfish and mashed potatoes thoroughly mixed with cooked red beets chopped fine. Mold into balls, brown in the fat of salt pork, and garnish with the crisp bits of fried pork.

FISH A LUCULLUS.

BY MRS. JOHN W. NOBLE.
(Wife of the Secretary of the Interior.)

SLICE one middling-sized onion and fry it with one ounce of butter until it turns yellow; add three or four pounds of fish (bass, pike, trout, or any fish having a firm and compact flesh); add, also, two carrots, two onions and one leek (all sliced), four stalks of parsley, one of thyme, one clove of garlic if to the taste, a bay-leaf, one clove, six peppercorns and salt; cover the whole with cold water; set on a good but not brisk fire, and boil gently for about two hours. If the water is boiling away, add some, then strain and use.

Lizabeth H. Noble

FISH CHOWDER.

BY MRS. JOHN SHERMAN.
(Wife of Senator from Ohio.)

BOIL a codfish (any fish will answer) weighing about five pounds; take out all the bones, and season lightly with pepper and salt; take a quart of milk, put in five small onions, a bunch of thyme and parsley, a teaspoonful of salt, one-half teaspoonful of white pepper, and one-half teaspoonful of grated nutmeg; simmer all together for fifteen minutes, and then strain. Then return to the fire, and add one-quarter pound flour, one-quarter pound butter, and yolks of two eggs. Stir until it thickens, but do not let it get too thick. Then in your baking-dish put alternate layers of sauce and fish, having the sauce on top and bottom. Grate bread crumbs and Parmessan cheese over the top; place in a moderate oven, and bake half an hour.

C. S. Sherman

DEVILED CRABS.

BY MRS. M. S. QUAY.
(Wife of Senator from Pennsylvania.)

BOIL one dozen crabs twenty minutes; when cold, pick. Three eggs, well beaten, two tablespoonfuls Vienna bread crumbs, four of melted butter, one of olive oil, one tablespoonful of chopped parsley. Season with salt and pepper. Mix all together, using cream to moisten, and put back in the shells, which should be clean and dry. Dip in beaten eggs and Vienna bread crumbs and fry in hot lard to cover.

Agnes B Quay

BROILED OYSTERS ON TOAST.

BY MRS. C. K. DAVIS.
(Wife of Senator from Minnesota.)

TAKE the largest oysters obtainable. Brush the wire oyster-broiler with softened butter, lay in the oysters and broil over a hot fire two or three minutes, basting once on each side with butter-brush. Dish side by side on a long slice of buttered toast in a dish. Garnish with lemon and parsley.

Mrs. C. K. Davis

BAKED FISH.

BY MRS. J. E. CAMPBELL.
(Wife of the Governor of Ohio.)

CLEAN, rinse and wipe dry a white fish, or any fish, weighing three or four pounds; rub the fish inside and out with salt and pepper, fill with a stuffing made like that for poultry, but drier; tie the fish up and put in a hot pan with some drippings and a lump of butter, dredge with flour and lay over the fish a few slices of thin salt pork or bits of butter, and bake an hour and a half, basting occasionally.

Elizabeth Campbell

STEWED OYSTERS, ETC.

BY MRS. ROSWELL P. FLOWER.
(Wife of Representative from New York.)

BLANCH a dozen oysters in their own liquor; salt and remove the oysters; add a tablespoonful of butter, the juice of half a lemon, a gill of cream and a tablespoonful of flour. Beat up the yolk of one egg while the sauce is simmering; add the egg, and simmer the whole until it thickens. Place the oysters in a hot dish, pour the sauce over them, sprinkle a little chopped parsley on top, and send to table. To blanch an oyster is to cook it till it puffs up.

DRESSING FOR ONE FISH.

Half a pound of butter, half can tomatoes; stew for one-half hour; one tablespoonful of walnut catsup, one tablespoonful of Worcestershire sauce, or two tablespoonfuls of chow-chow; add sliced lemon, very thin.

Sarah M. Flower

BAKED SHAD.

BY MRS. R. M. LA FOLLETTE.
(Wife of Representative from Wisconsin.)

SELECT a fresh roe shad, clean and prepare carefully, splitting it at the breast rather than the back. Fill it with any good dressing, oyster filling preferred, first salting lightly inside and out; sew up the slit and lay the fish in a dripping-pan; butter it generously and add a little water. Let it bake about half an hour in a moderate oven, or till it is thoroughly browned. Lift it out on a dish, draw out the stitches, and serve hot with any kind of fish sauce preferred.

Belle C. La Follette

SCALLOPED OYSTERS.

BY MRS. J. R. M'KEE.
(Daughter of the President.)

BOIL the macaroni soft, put a layer into a baking-dish, cover with oysters, pepper, salt and butter, then another layer of macaroni, then a layer of oysters until the dish is filled. Bake.

Yours cordially,
Mary Harrison McKee

CODFISH FAKE.

BY COL. GILBERT A. PIERCE.
(Senator from North Dakota.)

TAKE some codfish—old salt fish, the saltiest you can buy, and take all you can get. Then boil it well, just as long as you want to; boil all the salt out of it, or as much as you can get out. Of course you boil this in water. The gravy is the most important part. You boil some plain water and put in butter—lots of butter—and flour; but be careful about flour, not to get too much. The gravy wants to be of a consistency between Washington milk and real cream. Have a big pot of boiled potatoes, boiled with their jackets on. For one person take four of these big mealy potatoes, take jackets off and mash very fine all over a big dinner-plate. Spread this area of potato with the fine codfish, leaving no part uncovered. Next, pour gravy over the entire surface of fish. Pour copiously, after which black pepper must be used, very black pepper, which lights up the gravy and gives expression to the entire dish. The codfish is now ready for eating, and if made with strict regard to recipe will not fail of a result.

TERRAPIN.

BY HON. THOMAS F. BAYARD.
(Late Secretary of State.)

TAKE two "counts" and boil in the shell; after allowing them to cool, remove the shell, take out the gall-bladder, and cut the terrapin in good-sized pieces; put in a chafing-dish, and to this add small cupful of rich cream, half a pound of butter, and a couple wineglassfuls of sherry or madeira. Most epicures prefer madeira because of its richer flavor. No one has ever tasted terrapin prepared after this recipe who is not a convert to its excellence.

FISH CHOWDER.

BY CAPT. G. E. THORNTON.
(Pay Director, U. S. Navy.)

TAKE one-half pound fat salt pork, cut into slices and fry out well. Slice four large onions and fry in the pork-fat until they are a light brown. Stir constantly to prevent burning, and thus making the chowder bitter. Put this into a pot with three quarts of boiling water, and let it boil twenty minutes. Skim out the pieces of pork and onion and add ten potatoes, sliced, not too thin, and boil twenty minutes; then add two pounds of solid fish-shred and boil ten minutes, if the fish is not cooked; add salt and pepper to taste. When cooked stir in slowly a thickening made of two tablespoonfuls of farina mixed in cold milk, and let it boil up once only. Put the pot back on the fire, and, after letting it stand a few moments, skim off the scum which will rise to the top, and serve. Recipe sufficient for eight persons.

TO PREPARE A TURKEY FOR CHRISTMAS DINNER.

BY MRS. STEPHEN J. FIELD.
(Wife of Associate Justice of the Supreme Court.)

THE turkey should be cooped up and fed well some time before Christmas. Three days before it is slaughtered it should have an English walnut forced down its throat three times a day, and a glass of sherry once a day. The meat will be deliciously tender, and have a fine nutty flavor.

BAKED CHICKEN.

BY MRS. THOMAS B. REED.
(Wife of the Speaker of the House of Representatives.)

SELECT a tender fowl, if possible—to have it fresh is imperative; dress it carefully; fill with any desired dressing; thrust the legs through the hole made in drawing it at the back; pinion the wings close to the sides; dredge with salt and a little pepper, and place in a dripping-pan with about one-half teacup of water. Put it in a moderate oven and do not disturb it for fifteen or twenty minutes. Then begin to baste it, repeating the process frequently till testing with a fork shows that it is done. If it browns too rapidly, turn another pan over it at the last. Serve with gravy. If the chicken is tough, parboil slowly till partly done, and put to bake with the broth.

Susan P. Reed.

YOUNG ROAST PIG FOR CHRISTMAS.

BY MRS. JAMES S. CLARKSON.
(Wife of the First Assistant Postmaster-General.)

PROCURE a fine young pig not over six or eight weeks old. See that the flesh is firm and pink and the eyes healthy and clear. Have it neatly dressed, leaving the head intact and the feet and tail *au naturelle*. Prepare a dressing of breadcrumbs, three eggs well beaten (yolks and whites together), half a teacupful of butter, onions to taste, a slight pinch of powdered sage, a handful of large raisins, and salt and pepper to suit the palate; rub the inside of the pig with salt and pepper, and lay along the backbone slices of salt pork, as the young meat needs the relish of the smoked bacon. Fill with the dressing, which is well mixed with water and a few spoonfuls of rich cream, and sew firmly together with cord. Put it in a large baking-pan, with the knees turned under and a small cob in the mouth to keep it open. Put a little water in the pan and leave it to the mercies of a moderate oven for twenty minutes, when the basting must begin and be continued at regular intervals until it is brown and tender. When ready to a turn place on the platter on its knees; put on his back a little Chinese doll on a saddle of blue satin, with reins of smilax, and for a bit an ear of popcorn; wire the cue of the doll so it will stand out straight, and you will be astonished at the rate of speed which his pigship is making across the table. Garnish the dish with holly and mistletoe, and if you have a lot of merry children about you will be well paid for your trouble in watching the pleasure which this jaunty little race-horse will give them.

Anna Howell Clarkson.

A SADDLE OF MUTTON.

BY MRS. J. LOWRIE BELL.
(Wife of Superintendent of Railway Mail Service.)

SEND for your butcher about November 1, and order him to take a week in selecting your Christmas mutton. If you take the shoulder too, you can get the whole for 18 cents per pound. Wash the saddle, wrap it in heavy muslin and hang it where the temperature can be kept below freezing. Every few days the cloth should be wet with vinegar. After six weeks' care it is just ready for the Christmas dinner, and should be washed in salt and water, placed in a large pan and basted frequently. A safe rule for roasting is twenty minutes to the pound. Currant jelly should be served with it. The delicious flavor depends in part on the carver. He should cut the slices very thin, and parallel with the backbone.

BARBACUED MUTTON.

BY MRS. ROGER Q. MILLS.
(Wife of Representative from Texas.)

TAKE a nice, tender forequarter or only the ribs of lamb or mutton. Cut it across three or four times to break the bones, so as to carve easily. Put it in a flat stove pan, or, better, on a broiler in front of the fire. Let it broil slowly. Take a pint of vinegar, add to it two tablespoonfuls of red pepper (pods cut up fine much the best), teaspoonful black pepper, salt to taste and two tablespoonfuls of butter. Keep this hot. Make a sponge of a piece of soft cloth, and all the time the meat is cooking mop it with dressing. When ready pour on the rest of the dressing and serve hot.

Mrs R. Q. Mills —

ROAST TURKEY.

BY MRS. THOS. J. HENDERSON.
(Wife of Representative from Illinois.)

TAKE one loaf of bread, scald it with boiling water; take the liver of the turkey, one pint of oysters, two stalks of celery, one raw egg, two-thirds of a cup of butter; mix and chop together very fine. Season with salt, pepper and a little nutmeg; dredge the turkey with flour, and put small bits of butter on the breast, with pepper and salt. Roast from two and a half to three hours; baste frequently while roasting it.

H. B. Henderson.

ROAST BEEF.

BY MRS W. D. BYNUM.
(Wife of Representative from Indiana.)

THE best pieces for roasting are the tenderloin, sirloin and rib-pieces—the sixth, seventh and eighth ribs are best. If you get a rib-piece, have the butcher take out the bone, and roll and skewer the meat in shape. If there is much fat on the surface, cover the roast with a paste of flour and water. This should be removed half an hour before the meat is done. Have the oven rather hot, if you like beef rare, and allow twelve minutes to the pound. If preferred well done, have the oven moderate and cook a longer time. Serve with gravy.

ROAST VEAL.

BY MRS. ALFRED C. HARMER.
(Wife of Representative from Pennsylvania.)

TAKE a leg of veal and remove the bone, making several incisions in the thick part beside. Make a stuffing of crackers, eggs, chopped fat pork, sage, pepper and salt, enough to fill the holes. Bind and skewer carefully together. Then take very thick and fat pickled pork, cut it into slices as thin as you can with a very sharp knife, and cover the veal entirely over with it, binding it securely with strips of muslin (cords would cut the meat as it cooked); put it in a deep dish and set it in a steamer; let it steam three hours. Remove it, and put it in the oven in a dripping-pan with the gravy in the dish, and bake it an hour and a half or two hours more—according to size, basting it constantly. Peel off the fat and serve hot.

Sarah E. Harmer.

BAKED HAM.

BY MRS. GEO T. BARNES.
(Wife of Representative from Georgia.)

TAKE a ham weighing eight or ten pounds. Prepare as for boiling, washing and scraping it well. Then take one pint of flour and make a thick, stiff batter, and cover the ham all over with it. Place it in a baking-pan raised on three muffin-rings, and bake fifteen minutes for every pound, in an oven heated as for turkey. When it is done, peel off all the crust, including the skin of the ham, and when it is cold slice it in thin slices.

Mrs Geo. T. Barnes

ROAST TURKEY.

BY MRS. GEO. W. SMITH,
(Wife of Representative from Illinois.)

FIRST stew the fowl slowly for half an hour; then fill with any desired dressing. Secure the legs; run a skewer through the wings, fastening them to the body; skewer the neck fast to the body underneath, and tie all securely with twine. Place it in a covered roasting-pan that will retain all the steam, and therefore all the flavor; pour the liquor over it and baste it once in a while, but not so frequently as if in an open pan. By the time the turkey is nicely browned it will be done through, as the covered pan prevents it from coloring prematurely. Serve with giblet gravy and cranberry sauce.

GIBLET GRAVY.

Boil the giblets for two hours; then take them out, chop the gizzard and heart, braid the liver, and put them back again. Thicken with one tablespoonful of flour wet with cold water, season with salt and pepper. Let this simmer one hour longer, and when you dish the turkey turn the drippings into the gravy, boil up once, and send to the table.

Make all the gravy for poultry this way, omitting the chopped gizzard in chicken gravy.

Elizabeth M. Smith

STUFFED HAM.

BY MRS. T. C. CATCHINGS.
(Wife of Representative from Mississippi.)

SELECT a very fine quality of ham, a newly-cured ham if possible. Boil it slowly until it is so well done that the bone can be removed. (It can be taken out or not, as you please.) For the dressing take one pint toasted bread or crackers, two tablespoons of celery seed, one-half tablespoon of black pepper, one-half tablespoon of spice, one-half tablespoon of cloves, one tablespoon of mustard, three tablespoons of sugar, six yolks of eggs, some good pickle and two or three onions chopped fine, a little vinegar; mix all well. Make incisions to the bone all over the ham and press the dressing into the incisions, forcing it through the lean part of the ham; then spread the remainder of the dressing over the top of the ham and glaze with white of egg. Bake slowly for about an hour.

Florence S. Catchings.

ROAST DUCK.

BY MRS. JOHN J. INGALLS.
(Wife of the President *pro tem.* of the Senate.)

ROAST two wild ducks. When cold carve nicely, rejecting the wings. Put into a stew-pan one pint of water, one pint of tomatoes, strained; one tablespoonful of onion juice, salt and pepper to taste. As soon as this boils up throw in the sliced duck and boil 15 minutes. At the last moment thicken with a little cornstarch and throw in two dozen olives. When all is well heated through serve at once. This is delicious when well prepared.

HOW TO COOK ORTOLANS.

BY MRS. J. E. CAMPBELL.
(Wife of the Governor of Ohio.)

ROLL an oyster in melted butter, then in bread crumbs seasoned with pepper and salt, and put into each bird before roasting. Baste with butter and water three times during the twelve minutes of cooking, and after putting them on crisp slices of toast, baste again freely with butter.

Elizabeth Campbell

CANNED-CORN PATTIES.

BY MRS. WM. WINDOM.
(Wife of the Secretary of the Treasury.)

TAKE one can of best sweet corn and chop fine in a chopping-tray. Add two beaten eggs, to which has been added two tablespoonfuls of milk, a tablespoonful of salt, a half-tablespoonful of pepper, and two even tablespoonfuls of flour. Beat well and fry on a griddle in a tablespoonful of mixed lard and butter, dropping one spoonful for each patty. Fry brown on both sides and serve hot.

Ellen T. Windom

STEAM BROWN BREAD.

BY MRS. W. H. H. MILLER.
(Wife of the Attorney-General of the United States.)

TWO cups of corn meal, one cup of wheat flour, one cup of either rye or graham, one-half cup of New Orleans molasses, one pint of sour milk, two scant teaspoons of soda; salt. Boil in mold three hours. Serve hot.

Gertrude A. Miller

GRAHAM GEMS.

BY MRS. W. H. H. MILLER.
(Wife of the Attorney-General of the United States.)

ONE quart of flour; rub into this lard about the size of an ordinary egg; two heaping tablespoons of brown sugar, two heaping teaspoonfuls of baking powder; wet up with water till it cleans from the spoon. Bake in a dripping-pan well greased, dropping them in a spoonful at a time a little way apart. Bake in a moderate oven about fifteen or twenty minutes. The same batter in a gem-pan is not nearly so good.

Gertrude A. Miller

BREAD.

BY MRS. JAS. F. WILSON.
(Wife of Senator from Iowa.)

TAKE one gallon of sour milk; scald until whey separates from curd; then strain through colander and set away to cool; when cool enough stir in flour until stiff; then put in one-half cup yeast and let rise over night. In the morning stir in one small teaspoonful soda dissolved in water; then stir in one tablespoonful of lard and two of sugar. Mix very stiff; then let it rise one-half hour and knead down in pan. When it rises again make into six loaves.

Mrs. J. F. Wilson

CORN PONE.

BY MRS. J. K. JONES.
(Wife of Senator from Arkansas.)

INTO one quart of meal put one teaspoonful soda and sift well. Break into this two eggs and salt to taste. Mix all with clabbered milk, beating it well. Pour into a hot pan greased with good, sweet hog's lard. Bake in a hot oven, much hotter than needed for flour bread. Serve when browned. Baking powder and sweet milk can be substituted for clabber and soda.

Mrs. J. K. Jones

CORN MUFFINS.

BY MRS. CHAS. F. MANDERSON.
(Wife of Senator from Nebraska.)

ONE-HALF cup (small measure) Indian meal, one-half cup (large measure) flour, one cup milk, pinch of sugar, pinch of salt, heaping teaspoon baking powder, two eggs, butter size of walnut. First beat well together yolks of eggs, butter, sugar and salt; then add milk, little at a time, beating well; then corn meal; then flour with baking powder sifted in; last stir into mixture whites of eggs, beaten stiff. Put into gem-pans smoking hot and bake in rather a hot oven.

R. S. Manderson

EGG BREAD.

BY MRS. WM. B. BATE.
(Wife of Senator from Tennessee.)

TWO cups of corn meal, three cups of buttermilk, one tablespoon of lard, one teaspoon of soda, one teaspoon of salt, one egg. Eat hot with fresh buttermilk.

*Mrs Wm B. Bate —
Nashville —
Tenn —*

SWEDISH TIMBALES.

BY MRS. J. C. S. BLACKBURN.
(Wife of Senator from Kentucky.)

ONE pint of flour, one half-pint of sweet milk, three eggs, two tablespoonfuls of salad oil, scant teaspoonful of salt. Stir the flour and milk to a perfectly smooth batter, add oil and salt; then the eggs, whipped very light. If too thick, add more milk until right consistency.

Terese G. Blackburn

BREAKFAST CAKES.

BY MRS. JOHN C. SPOONER.
(Wife of Senator from Wisconsin.)

ONE teacup of milk, one coffeecup of flour, one egg, all beaten together; tablespoon of butter; salt. To be baked in iron pans. The secret of success in these cakes is the moderate oven.

Annie Main Spooner

MILK BREAD.

BY MRS. NELSON DINGLEY, JR.
(Wife of Representative from Maine.)

ONE quart of cold boiled milk, one large spoonful of lard, one even tablespoon of sugar, one tablespoon of salt, one yeast cake dissolved in warm water. Raise over night.

Mrs. N. Dingley Jr.

BEATEN BISCUIT.

BY MRS. JAS. H. BLOUNT.
(Wife of Representative from Georgia.)

TO a quart of flour take a large tablespoonful of lard and a teaspoonful of salt. Mix with cold sweet milk and water—half and half—into a stiff dough; lay it on a marble or wooden board, and beat it with a club of hickory or poplar wood till the dough becomes blistered and nearly as soft as yeast-powder dough. Roll it half an inch thick, cut out with a biscuit-cutter, prick with a kitchen fork three rows of holes clear through to the bottom. Bake in a moderate oven, and when done, allow them to remain a few moments longer, to brown a little more thoroughly. Break open and butter.

E. W. Blount

SALT-RISING BREAD.

BY MRS. T. R. STOCKDALE.
(Wife of Representative from Mississippi.)

TAKE a quart of milk and water, equal portions. Stir in flour to make a stiff batter, that will not run from the spoon, but drops like drop-cake batter. Add a teaspoonful of salt; put it in a warm place; let it stand three or four hours, and then, if water rises on the top, stir in a little more flour. After it rises make up your dough just as you would ordinary bread, using the rising instead of yeast, adding about a gill of milk or water and a little more salt, and lard about the size of an egg; knead it well and put it into well-greased pans and let it rise. Be careful not to jar it while rising. Bake the same as yeast bread.

Mrs. T. R. Stockdale

JOHNNY CAKES.

BY MRS. W. O. ARNOLD.
(Wife of Representative from Rhode Island.)

ONE cup of Indian meal, a pinch of salt, butter the size of a walnut; pour over this enough boiling water to make a stiff batter, after being well stirred. Set for three or four minutes in a dish of boiling water; then thin with sweet milk until the batter drops easily from the spoon. Put on a hot, buttered griddle in spoonfuls, and when brown, turn them over and brown the other side. This will make six good-sized cakes. Water may be used in place of the milk, but the cakes will not brown so nicely in that case.

Yours respectfully
Mary A. Arnold.

SWEET CORN BREAD.

BY MRS. ALBERT G. THOMPSON.
(Wife of Representative from Ohio.)

TWO cups Indian meal, two cups "loppered" or buttermilk, one cup flour, one-half cup New Orleans molasses, one tablespoonful lard, one teaspoonful salt, one teaspoonful soda. Stir meal, flour, milk and salt together well. Dissolve soda in a little warm water and melt lard. Add both to molasses; beat quickly and turn both into the batter at once, stirring hard. Turn all into a well-buttered farina-kettle or pudding-mold. Boil one and a half hours. Remove cover and place in oven to brown. When done rub the top with a little butter, replace cover and let stand about five minutes on table. Turn out and serve warm, using sharp, thin knife to slice.

Ella A. Thompson

COMMON BISCUIT.

BY MRS. A. G. CARUTH.
(Wife of Representative from Kentucky.)

SIFT well about a quart of flour into a bowl; stir into the middle of it two heaping teaspoonfuls of Royal baking powder, an even teaspoon of salt, and a heaping tablespoon of lard, in the order directed. Have a pint of cold sweet milk, make a hole in the center of the flour, pour in the milk and mix quickly with enough flour to make a soft dough. Roll on a biscuit-board with the rest of the flour till you have a sheet about one-inch thick; cut out and place in a dry pan, setting closely together, so that they will rise upward without spreading. Put into a quick oven on the bottom and bake to a light brown. Serve immediately.

Mrs. A. G. Caruth
Louisville,
Ky.

GREEN-CORN FRITTERS.

BY MRS. WM. J. CONNELL.
(Wife of Representative from Nebraska.)

CUT through each row of kernels of sweet corn with the point of a sharp knife, then with the back of the knife press out the pulp. To one pint of corn-pulp add two well-beaten eggs, a little salt and pepper, and enough flour to keep the corn and eggs together. Fry in small cakes on a buttered griddle, browning well on each side.

Mrs. W. J. Connell.

FRIED CAKES.

BY MRS. GEO. H. BRICKNER,
(Wife of Representative from Wisconsin.)

MEASURE one cup each of milk and granulated sugar into a mixing-bowl; stir till dissolved; beat three eggs well and stir in; take two quarts of flour and three heaping teaspoons of baking powder, sifted together; mix the whole into a soft dough, using as little flour in manipulating it as possible. Cut into rings and fry in very hot lard. Mixing the sugar and milk together first keeps the dough from soaking grease, and avoiding the use of a great deal of flour in working with the dough makes the cakes puffy and delicate.

Mrs G. H. Brickner,

WAFFLES.

BY MRS. ALBERT C. THOMPSON.
(Wife of Representative from Ohio.)

ONE pint sour milk, one heaping pint flour, one tablespoonful melted butter, one level teaspoonful soda, three eggs. Stir milk into flour; add melted butter and yolks of eggs. Beat well and add soda dissolved in a little warm water. Stir rapidly and then add the whites of eggs beaten to a froth.

Ellen A. Thompson

LOAF BREAD.

BY MRS. DANIEL M. RANSDELL.
(Wife of United States Marshal for District of Columbia.)

THREE quarts of fine white flour well sifted; one-half pint of good fresh yeast, one tablespoon of lard, one tablespoon of salt, warm water enough to make a dough. Dissolve the lard and salt in warm water; then add the yeast, then the flour, gradually, stirring it with a spoon; set it to rise in a warm place over night. In the morning take part of the dough and mold it into rolls for breakfast. Then knead the rest thoroughly on a pie-board, dividing it into three parts, and kneading them separately. Lay them in buttered tins, either separately or all in one long one, set in a warm place, and let it rise almost to the top of the pans. Bake for about half an hour, keeping the oven closed for ten or fifteen minutes before venturing to open the door.

Mary C. Ransdell.

CREAM TOAST.

BY MISS L. S. SWAN.
(Sister-in-law of Senator Morrill, of Vermont.)

ALWAYS bake one loaf to be used especially for toasting; have it shapely, and bake it so thoroughly that it will be neither soggy nor full of holes. Stale or dried bread should never be used. Cut into slices of medium thickness, brown the bread until it matches the crust in color, butter and cover with a hot cream dressing, which has just been allowed to come to a boil. Toast made with care is the daintiest breakfast dish conceivable.

L. S. Swan.

SAUSAGE ROLLS.

BY MRS. BENJAMIN HARRISON.
(Wife of the President.)

EXECUTIVE MANSION,
WASHINGTON.

Sausage Rolls

Make a light biscuit dough — (made with milk) & let it raise over night. In the morning roll it out thin, & cut into shape with a biscuit cutter. In the center of each place a roll of sausage the size of a good sized Hickory nut & roll it up in the dough —. After letting them stand in the pan for a few minutes. bake & serve hot

These rolls are also good cold. & when children we used to have them to take to school for our luncheon in bad weather

Caroline Scott Harrison

LEMON OMELET.

BY MRS. M. S. QUAY.
(Wife of Senator from Pennsylvania.)

WHITES of six eggs, yolks of three, juice of half a lemon, three tablespoonfuls powdered sugar. Grease a quart baking-dish with butter. Now beat the whites to a very stiff froth, beat the yolks, add them carefully to the whites, then the sugar and juice of lemon, stir carefully and quickly heap into baking-dish; powder over with sugar and put into the oven. Bake fifteen minutes, or until a golden brown, and serve hot.

Agnes B Quay

MISSISSIPPI BAKED HASH.

BY MRS. JAS. Z. GEORGE.
(Wife of Senator from Mississippi.)

HASH the cold beef fine; take stale wheaten bread, biscuit or any other kind, and crumble a quantity equal to the hashed meat; add one egg well beaten, half a cup of sweet milk, a little salt and pepper, thyme or other flavoring; mix well; then melt an even tablespoon of butter and stir it into the mixture. Stir it up thoroughly and then pour it into the buttered pan and bake in a hot oven.

Mrs. E. B. George

BEEF COLLAR.

BY MRS. JAS. Z. GEORGE.
(Wife of Senator from Mississippi.)

TAKE a piece of flank, lay it in salt a day or two, according to the weather. Then wash and cut off all the loose fat and gristle; score it on the inside; season with a little pepper, allspice and nutmeg; roll it up tightly in a cloth, with ends well secured, and boil from six to eight hours, according to weight, not letting it boil violently. Set it away to cool; slice thin and serve cold. Excellent for luncheon.

Mrs. E. B. George

RELISH FOR LUNCH.

BY MRS. THOS. B. REED.
(Wife of the Speaker of the House of Representatives.)

PLACE some Boston crackers in the oven to heat. Then split them and butter lightly while hot; over this sprinkle grated cheese, having the cheese rather dry, and a pinch of cayenne pepper. Set them on the grate of the oven, and let them brown. Serve hot.

This is a dish much esteemed in our family.

Susan P. Reed.

SWEETBREADS AND MUSHROOMS.

BY MRS. J. N. HUSTON.
(Wife of the Treasurer of the United States.)

TAKE a nice, large pair of sweetbreads, trim off the ears and soak in salt water for an hour; wash in cold water, and boil until done. When cold, cut into small pieces; take half a jar of French button mushrooms, slice and put them in half pint water and boil five minutes; add the sweetbreads and boil ten minutes. Rub a tablespoon of flour in a large piece of fresh, sweet butter, size of an egg, until smooth, and stir into it a half cup of cream; pour into mushrooms and sweetbreads, having first seasoned them with salt and pepper, and let it boil five minutes. Serve immediately in a hot dish.

Mrs J. N. Huston

CHICKEN CROQUETS.

BY MRS. A. W. GREELY.
(Wife of the Chief of the Signal Service.)

ONE large chicken, roasted, one pair small sweetbreads, and a little of the soft bread dressing with which the chicken has been stuffed, chopped fine together. Make a drawn butter of one pint of cream, in which an onion has stood until the cream is ready to boil; one-half cup of butter and sufficient flour to make a thick sauce. Season the chicken mixture highly with chopped parsley, the juice of half a lemon, salt and red pepper—chili colorado, not cayenne. Mix with the drawn butter and heat thoroughly, stirring constantly. When cool form the croquets with cracker dust, roll in beaten egg, then in cracker dust, and fry.

Very cordially yours,
Henrietta N. Greely

PRESSED CHICKEN.

BY MRS. THOS. J. HENDERSON.
(Wife of Representative from Illinois.)

BOIL the chicken until very tender; remove the meat from the bones and pick it in small pieces with a fork; put a layer of hard-boiled eggs and a layer of chicken into a mold; boil the broth to a jelly and pour it over the chicken; season with salt and pepper. Set it on the ice to cool. To be cut in slices; garnish with parsley.

H. B. Henderson.

VEAL LOAF.

BY MRS. J. G. SAWYER.
(Wife of Representative from New York.)

ONE and a half pints cold veal well minced, one pint powdered crackers, one teacup milk, one-half teacup butter, two eggs. Stir veal and cracker dust together, seasoning with salt and pepper; beat eggs in milk and add one-half pound of butter, melted; mix all together and pour in buttered baking-dish; press down until smooth and put rest of butter on top; cover and bake one-half hour; remove cover and brown. Serve hot in dish, or sliced when cold.

Mrs J. G. Sawyer

CURRIED MUTTON CHOPS.

BY MRS. JOS. E. WASHINGTON.
(Wife of Representative from Tennessee.)

GET the best rib chops, and have them cut about an inch thick. Put them in melted butter several hours before cooking. Half an hour before they are to be eaten slip the pan in which they are with the butter into the stove and melt the butter a second time. Then dip them into the following preparation: A loaf of stale bread rolled and sifted until it is like meal, the yellows of six hard-boiled eggs, three teaspoonfuls chopped parsley, two teaspoonfuls of grated onion, one teaspoonful of thyme, one teaspoonful of sweet marjoram, salt, pepper (black and red), etc., and two tablespoonfuls of curry powder. Mix this thoroughly together. When the chops have been rolled in this put them in a deep pan and add the melted butter and Port or Madeira wine enough to keep them from burning. Cook twenty minutes, basting frequently; cut heart-shaped papers, butter them well and wrap a chop in each, folding the edges carefully. Slip in the stove for two minutes, and serve very hot.

Mary B. Washington

VEAL FRICANDEAU.

BY MRS. A. T. BLISS.
(Wife of Representative from Michigan.)

THREE and a half pounds chopped veal, one pound chopped salt pork, three slices of bread and butter, two eggs, pepper, a little thyme or sage Pack in a dish; bake for three hours. To be eaten cold.

P. S. The bread is to be crumbled up fine, and mixed thoroughly with the rest, the same as any other loaf.

Allaseba M. Bliss

CREAM CHICKEN.

BY MRS. MARK S. BREWER.
(Wife of Representative from Michigan.)

FOUR chickens, four sweetbreads, three cans mushrooms. Boil chicken until tender, and cut as for salad (removing all the skin); boil sweetbread and chop very fine; chop mushroom rather coarsely; mix all together and bake in a dish, with alternate layers of the above and the cream dressing given below, putting bread crumbs, pieces of butter and a little cream over the top before baking. Bake twenty minutes.

CREAM DRESSING FOR ABOVE.

One and a half pint sweet cream, three tablespoonfuls flour, four tablespoonfuls butter, one-fourth of a grated nutmeg, one very small onion, grated, a little cayenne pepper and salt to taste. Scald cream, rub butter and flour together; cook all together until the consistency of custard.

(For 25 people.)

Mrs. M. S. Brewer.

PLAIN OMELET.

BY MRS W. E. MASON.
(Wife of Representative from Illinois.)

FOUR eggs, whites and yolks beaten separately; four tablespoons milk, scant teaspoonful salt; cut the yolks into whites with a fork, lightly. Pan very hot; one tablespoon butter; pour omelet in, shake leisurely over hottest part of the fire five minutes, then put in the oven a moment to set it; run knife round the side of the pan, fold over; turn out on a hot dish.

Edith J. W. Mason

MEAT SOUFFLÉ.

BY MRS. ORREN C. MOORE.
(Wife of Representative from New Hampshire.)

TAKE a smooth, white sauce with two tablespoonfuls of butter, one heaping tablespoonful of flour, and two-thirds cup of milk. Season with chopped parsley and onion juice. While hot add the beaten yolks of two eggs and one cup of chopped meat (chicken, veal, fresh tongue, boiled ham or lamb) and boil one minute. When cool stir in the well-beaten whites of the eggs. Bake in a buttered dish twenty minutes, and serve immediately. If for lunch, serve with mushroom sauce.

VEAL LOAF.

BY MRS. J. A. PICKLER.
(Wife of Representative from South Dakota.)

FOUR pounds veal chopped very fine at butcher's, one small slice fresh pork, one dozen soda crackers powdered, four eggs. Mix all together and add pepper and salt to taste. Bake in shallow pan two hours. Slice when cold.

Mrs Alice M. A. Pickler.

BAKED OMELET.

BY MRS. GEO. H. BRICKNER.
(Wife of Representative from Wisconsin.)

FOUR eggs beaten separately, one cup of sweet milk, one tablespoon of flour, a little salt; stir the whites in last of all; turn it into a well-buttered shallow pan and set in the oven about fifteen minutes. Serve immediately.

Mrs G. H. Brickner,

PUFF OMELET.

BY MRS. W. E. SIMONDS.
(Wife of Representative from Connecticut.)

HEAT one cupful of sweet milk, to which add a tablespoonful of corn starch, wet with a little cold milk; stir well together. When cool add four eggs, whites and yolks beaten separately; the yolks to be added first. Beat well together; salt and pepper to taste. Pour into a buttered dish, and bake in a quick oven. This is a delicious as well as ornamental breakfast dish.

Mrs. Wm E. Simonds
Hartford
Conn.

BOILING EGGS.

BY MRS. E. V. BROOKSHIRE.
(Wife of Representative from Indiana.)

PUT the eggs in the saucepan and cover with cold water; set it on the stove, and when the water boils the eggs are done.

Mrs E. V. Brookshire,

CHICKEN CROQUET.

BY MRS. H. C. M'CORMICK.
(Wife of Representative from Pennsylvania.)

HALF a pound of cold chicken chopped very fine. Fry a quarter of a grated onion with a tablespoonful of butter; stir the onion until it begins to get a little yellow; add one tablespoonful flour, stir a few minutes longer, then add a large coffeecup of broth in which the chicken has been boiled; then stir in the chopped chicken, with salt to taste; cook ten minutes, stirring all the time; a little grated nutmeg and cayenne pepper stirred in with the yolks of two eggs; give it one hard boil, and put on a dish to cool. When cold form with cracker dust and the white of an egg. Great care must be taken to have plenty of lard and boiling hot; drop them in carefully, three or four at a time. Cook them a light brown; take out with a perforated ladle and put them on a thick towel, that they may be perfectly dry and free from grease.

Ida H. M'Cormick
Williamsport
Pa.

BONED CHICKEN.

BY MISS JULIA DARLING STRONG.
(Daughter of ex-Associate Justice Strong, of the Supreme Court.)

CUT up a chicken into quite small pieces; skin it and pour over three pints of cold water. Boil it until the bones slip out of the meat easily; then take out all the meat; throw back the bones to boil in the liquor longer. Chop the meat with the rind of one lemon, having squeezed the juice into the boiling liquor. Put the meat, well-seasoned, into a jelly-mold, and when the liquor is boiled down fully one-half, strain it over the meat in the mold. Next morning turn out and serve with salad.

Julia Darling Strong

CHIPPED BEEF.

BY MISS L. S. SWAN.
(Sister-in-law of Senator Morrill, of Vermont.)

TAKE fine chipped beef and after picking it to shreds allow it to come to a boil in water enough to cover. The water should be hot when the beef is put in. Drain thoroughly, and cover with a dressing made of two cups of half cream and half milk. Stir in butter the size of a walnut, and when about to boil thicken with a tablespoonful of corn starch which has been made to a thin paste. Stir in slowly, so that it will not curdle. This makes a good dish for luncheon.

L. S. Swan.

DEVILED EGGS.

BY MISS L. S. SWAN.
(Sister-in-law of Senator Morrill, of Vermont.)

BOIL one dozen eggs hard, remove the shells and cut in halves lengthwise. Take out the yolks, mix them to a smooth paste with half a teaspoonful of mustard, salt and cayenne pepper to taste, and a generous teaspoonful of Worcestershire sauce. Fill the whites with this mixture and serve on a bed of lettuce leaves, which should be carefully selected.

L. S. Swan.

BROILED TOMATOES.

BY MRS. N. P. BANKS.
(Wife of Representative from Massachusetts.)

CUT them in half flatwise; put them skin down on a hot iron for a few minutes; season with a very little pepper, salt and sugar. Have slices of bread toasted a nice brown, and buttered; lay on them the broiled tomatoes, put half a teacup of cream into the dish around the toast, and set in the oven a few minutes before serving.

Mary P. Banks

MASHED POTATOES.

BY MRS. R. P. BLAND.
(Wife of Representative from Missouri.)

PARE the potatoes, cut into pieces and place immediately in cold water. Peachblow best. Take them out when prepared and turn on boiling water. Cook quickly just as the meal is ready. Empty water off, and let stand on the stove till perfectly dry; salt to taste, butter and cream as much as needed to make the right consistency. Serve immediately.

Mrs. R P Bland

MINCED CABBAGE.

BY MRS. ROSWELL P. FLOWER.
(Wife of Representative from New York.)

DRAIN boiled cabbage in the colander; put it in the chopping-tray and chop fine. For each quart of chopped cabbage put two teaspoonfuls of butter and one of flour in the fryingpan. As soon as smooth and hot put in the cabbage, which season well with salt and pepper, and, if you like it, two tablespoonfuls of vinegar. Stir constantly for five to eight minutes. When done heap on a dish, make smooth with a knife, and garnish with hard-boiled eggs.

Sarah M. Flower

CAULIFLOWER.

BY MRS. W. O. ARNOLD.
(Wife of Representative from Rhode Island.)

PUT a cauliflower in a dish of cold salted water, with the flower down, and let it soak for two hours. Tie in a cloth and put into boiling water with a little salt, and boil until a fork will penetrate the stem easily. If the cauliflower is fresh, it will boil in twenty minutes. When boiled, take it up carefully and put into a dish with the flower up. Have ready a sauce made of one-half pint of milk, a small pinch of salt, and one-half tablespoonful of butter. Let this come to a boil. Take a tablespoonful of flour mixed with a little cold milk, and stir into the boiling milk, and let it boil up once. Pour a little over the cauliflower when ready to serve, and serve the remainder in a gravy-boat. A tablespoonful of Worcestershire sauce may be added to the sauce if liked.

*Yours respectfully,
Mary A. Arnold.*

SPINACH.

BY MRS. JOHN M. FARQUHAR.
(Wife of Representative from New York.)

WASH the spinach in several waters, and keep in cold water until time to cook it. Then put it into boiling water enough to cover it, and add a little salt. Cover the pan and boil briskly till tender; it will sink when done. Take it from the water immediately, season it with butter, and cover with hard-boiled eggs in slices.

Mrs J. M. Farquhar,

LIMA BEANS.

BY MRS. MOSES D. STIVERS.
(Wife of Representative from New York.)

THE beans should be fresh and tender, but if they are not a pinch of soda in the first water will take away much of the strong taste. Parboil in water till they are half done, then turn off the water and renew from the teakettle, with just enough to finish cooking them. When they are thoroughly cooked season with butter first, letting it brown slightly, with a pinch of salt (unless the butter is quite salt), and a little sugar. After this has cooked into them thoroughly, pour in enough cream to make a little gravy; let it boil up once, and serve.

Mrs M E Stives

SCALLOPED SWEET POTATOES.

BY MRS. WM. J. CONNELL.
(Wife of Representative from Nebraska.)

CUT cold boiled sweet potatoes into quarter-inch slices and put them in a baking-dish. Sprinkle each layer slightly with sugar and dot with bits of butter. Bake until hot and slightly browned.

BAKED POTATOES.

BY MRS. JOS. M'KENNA,
(Wife of Representative from California.)

KNOWING how to bake and serve potatoes is a high art. Have a hot oven. Select potatoes of uniform size; wash well, and put moist into a clean oven. Do not open the oven, if you can avoid it, for half an hour. Try if they are done, in a towel. Serve immediately.

Amanda McKenna

ASPARAGUS.

BY MRS. BENJAMIN F. SHIVELY.
(Wife of Representative from Indiana.)

SELECT green asparagus; it is always sweeter and more tender than the white variety. After breaking off the hard part, take a sharp knife and strip off the outside skin, beginning at the cut end and drawing it upward as far as it will peel off. Put the stalks into a saucepan, sprinkle over them a little salt, and cover them with boiling water. Cook till tender, about twenty minutes. Season with cream, and thicken with a little flour rubbed into an equal quantity of butter. Serve hot.

Mrs Benjamin F. Shively.

GREEN PEAS.

BY MRS. J. B. WILLIAMS.
(Wife of Representative from Illinois.)

WASH before shelling, not after. When the peas are all shelled, take the tender pods and boil them ten or fifteen minutes in water enough to cover them; then skim out the pods and pour in the peas; boil them slowly about twenty minutes, then season with sweet cream and a little salt. Take care that there is not too much water; there should be about half a teacupful around them when they are thoroughly cooked, which must be seasoned and dished with the peas. When the peas are a trifle old, or not a very sweet variety, a spoonful of sugar will improve them.

Mrs. Minnie Shannon Williams.

MACARONI.

BY MRS. E. C. VENABLE.
(Wife of Representative from Virginia.)

BREAK into short pieces and boil in salted water till soft. Pour off the water and turn the macaroni into a dish with milk enough to keep it soft, a pinch of red pepper, a teaspoonful of mustard, and two tablespoonfuls of butter. Grate cheese over the top. Set it in the oven and let it brown. Serve hot.

Mrs E C Venable
Virginia

EGG-PLANT.

BY MRS. LEWIS F. WATSON.
(Wife of Representative from Pennsylvania.)

PARE the egg-plant and cut it into slices half an inch thick; put it to soak in cold water for two hours. This removes the black, bitter, disagreeable juice that is said to be unhealthy. Then press the slices between two plates, wipe them dry and boil them till soft; mash them smooth, season with salt, a little chopped parsley and a pinch of red pepper; add a few bread crumbs soaked in sweet cream; mix all thoroughly, pour into a buttered baking-dish, cover the top with some of the bread crumbs and bake half an hour. Serve hot.

Mrs Lewis F. Watson

GREEN VEGETABLES.

BY MRS. S. A. CRAIG.
(Wife of Representative from Pennsylvania.)

ALL green vegetables must be washed thoroughly in cold water, and then be dropped into water which has been salted and is just beginning to boil. There should be a tablespoonful of salt for every two quarts of water. If the water boils a long time before the vegetables are put in, it has lost all its gases, and the mineral ingredients are deposited on the bottom and sides of the kettle, so that the water is flat and tasteless, the vegetables will not look green and have a fine flavor. The time of boiling green vegetables depends very much on the age and how long they have been gathered. The younger and more freshly they are gathered, the more quickly they are cooked.

Mrs S. A. Craig.

STEWED CORN.

BY MISS PHŒBE W. COUZINS, LL.B.
(Ex-United States Marshal, Eastern District of Missouri.)

SPLIT the kernels of corn before removing from the cob, and in cutting off cut them several times through, leaving a large part on the cob to be scraped off, so as to make a fine mass of the whole. Take a pint of milk or cream, bring it to a boil, and put the corn in and boil slowly in a closed porcelain kettle for fifteen or twenty minutes, with a very little salt and sugar. It is better still when steamed.

Phoebe W. Couzins L.L.B.
Ex. U.S. Marshal

CHICKEN SALAD.

BY MRS. STANLEY MATTHEWS.
(Widow of Associate Justice of Supreme Court.)

TAKE the meat, free from skin and fat, of two large boiled chickens, cut in dice; with this mix thoroughly an equal quantity of good white crisp celery, cut in small pieces; three olives, chopped; two teaspoonfuls of capers; make a dressing of six spoonfuls of best imported olive oil, two tablespoonfuls of vinegar, two teaspoonfuls of salt, and a dash of red pepper; pour over the salad, and let it stand for several hours in the ice-box. Prepare a mayonnaise in the following manner: Break two eggs very carefully, and put the yolks into a soup-plate; then add, drop by drop, a pint bottle of best olive oil, stirring steadily one way with a silver fork. As the dressing thickens, thin with lemon juice, keeping it of the consistency of rich cream; add salt and cayenne pepper to taste. Make a mound of the chicken salad on a platter, pour over the mayonnaise and garnish with lettuce, olives, beets and carrots cut in fancy forms.

LOBSTER SALAD.

BY MRS. JOHN WANAMAKER.
(Wife of the Postmaster-General.)

SPLIT two good-sized, fine, freshly-boiled lobsters. Pick all the meat from out the shells, then cut it into one-inch lengths, equal pieces. Place it in a saucepan on the hot range, with one ounce of very good fresh butter. Season with one pinch of salt and half a saltspoonful of red pepper, adding two medium-sized sound truffles cut into small disk-shaped pieces. Cook for five minutes, then add a wineglassful of good Madeira wine. Reduce to one-half, which will take three minutes. Have three egg yolks in a bowl with half a pint of sweet cream; beat well together and add to it the lobster. Gently shuffle for two minutes longer, or until it thickens well. Pour it into a hot tureen and serve hot.

TOMATO SALAD.

BY MRS. EDWIN H. CONGER.
(Wife of Representative from Iowa.)

THREE heads of lettuce (medium sized), one can tomatoes without juice, or six fresh tomatoes; two cold boiled potatoes, one egg boiled hard; cut fine, mix together and season with salt.

DRESSING.

Two dessertspoonfuls of Durkee's salad dressing and three of sugar in teacup; fill cup with weak vinegar and pour over salad.

Sarah J. Conger.
Des Moines, Iowa

POTATO SALAD.

BY MRS. S. A. CRAIG.
(Wife of Representative from Pennsylvania.)

TAKE ten medium-sized cold potatoes and one small onion, chopped fine—the onion very fine; half dozen hard-boiled eggs, the white chopped fine; mash the yolks and add to them one teaspoon each of ground mustard and sugar, one tablespoon of melted butter, some salt and pepper. Rub all together well and put into the potatoes, with about four tablespoonfuls of Durkee's salad dressing and half a cup of vinegar. Then chop up stalks of celery to about the same quantity of the chopped potatoes and mix in. Slice a few more boiled eggs and lay on top, and garnish the edge of the dish with the celery-tops.

Mrs S. A. Craig.

COLD SLAW.

BY MRS. JASON B. BROWN.
(Wife of Representative from Indiana.)

CHOP the cabbage fine with chopping-knife; season with pepper, salt, mustard, sugar, (and celery seed if liked); boil some vinegar with a small lump of butter; beat the yolk of an egg and stir in quickly; then pour over the cabbage.

Mrs Jason B. Brown

CRAB SALAD.

BY MRS. J. R. M'KEE.
(Daughter of the President.)

BOIL one dozen crabs thirty minutes, adding a little salt to the water. When cold pick out the meat. Make a mayonnaise dressing as follows: Beat the yolks of two eggs, add pepper, salt and mustard and mix well together. Then slowly add half a pint of olive oil, or enough to thicken the dressing. If too thick, add a few drops of lemon juice or vinegar. Great care should be exercised in pouring the oil, as it will curdle if poured too fast. Now mix the crab meat and the mayonnaise together. Garnish a dish with crisp lettuce leaves or watercresses, place the crabs in the center, and serve.

*Yours cordially
Mary Harrison McKee*

CHICKEN SAUCE.

(Serves equally well for Pheasants, Quail, etc.)

BY MRS. J. W. NOBLE.
(Wife of the Secretary of the Interior.)

HEAPING tablespoonful butter, tablespoonful sifted flour; rub well together; one-half pint broth, two teaspoonfuls mushroom, two teaspoonfuls catsup, two tablespoonfuls cream, two teaspoonfuls lemon juice; put in to boil, stirring well; then add yolks of two eggs, beaten light, constantly stirring and never allowing to boil or it will curdle. When thickened by the eggs, serve, or place in hot water until wanted.

Lizabeth H. Noble

RELISH FOR COLD MEATS.

BY MRS. M. S. QUAY.
(Wife of Senator from Pennsylvania.)

FOUR large onions sliced and covered with vinegar. Let stand for two days. Mustard enough to thicken. One teaspoonful of sugar, one teaspoonful of salt and one of cayenne pepper. Put all together and pour vinegar over. Mix and boil five minutes.

Agnes B Quay

CHESTNUT STUFFING.

BY MRS. F. M. COCKRELL.
(Wife of Senator from Missouri.)

DRY bread crumbs, sweet herbs, chopped celery, a little grated nutmeg, pepper and salt. Put a small quantity of butter in a stewpan; when hot stir in a small minced onion, brown slightly and add the other ingredients, all thoroughly mixed, with two eggs and a little melted butter or stock. Cook through without browning. The chestnuts are put on the fire to burst their skin, boiled in salted water, and added to the dressing.

Anna Ewing Cockrell.

CHICKEN FILLING FOR PATTIES.

BY MRS. J. C. S. BLACKBURN.
(Wife of Senator from Kentucky.)

ONE pint of cream, one tablespoonful of flour, one pint cooked chicken cut in small bits, four tablespoonfuls of chopped mushroom, salt and pepper; put one-half of the cream on to boil; mix the other half with the flour, stir into the boiling cream; when this has boiled up once add chicken, mushrooms and seasoning.

CATSUP.

BY MRS. JOHN H. REAGAN.
(Wife of Senator from Texas.)

ONE peck of ripe tomatoes, peeled and sliced. Add six good-sized onions, sliced fine. Lay in a jar first a layer of tomatoes, then a layer of onions; add a little salt with each layer; let stand over night, then boil well, stirring almost constantly. When done add one pint of vinegar and two garlics chopped fine; add also red pepper, cinnamon, cloves, spice and ginger, all ground fine. Bottle for use.

NOTE.—This is especially appetizing for baked whitefish.

Mrs. John H. Reagan,

PICOLLI.

BY MRS. HENRY W. BLAIR.
(Wife of Senator from New Hampshire.)

ONE-HALF bushel tomatoes, one quart onions, three small peppers, three pounds sugar, one ounce mustard seed, two tablespoons each of cinnamon, cloves and allspice. Slice the tomatoes the night before, and put a layer of tomato an inch thick, then a good handful of fine salt, and continue until the whole are sliced. In the morning squeeze the fruit out and add the onions, cover with vinegar, and let it come to boil. Then drain off the vinegar, add a gallon of fresh vinegar and the rest of the ingredients. The pickle is much nicer if the spices are tied in thin muslin bags, and it is more delicate if the cinnamon is twice the amount of the cloves and allspice. Cook till tender.

Eliza N Blair

MUSHROOM SAUCE.

BY MRS. C. A. BERGEN.
(Wife of Representative from New Jersey.)

TAKE one tablespoonful of butter, melt it and stir into it while hot two tablespoonfuls of flour, sifting it gradually, and stirring constantly till smooth. Pour in a glass of milk or milk and cream, and stir continually till it boils; then drain off the liquor from a jar of French mushrooms, and taking the mixture from the fire put in the mushrooms, pepper and salt and steam it. Served with steak or chops.

Fannie Hurst Bergen
New Jersey

STRAWBERRY SAUCE.

BY MRS. W. D. OWEN.
(Wife of Representative from Indiana.)

BEAT to a cream one-half cup of sweet butter and two cups of powdered sugar; add a heaped half pint of strawberries. Mash the fruit thoroughly and beat it into the sauce.

(For any pudding.)

Mrs. W. D. Owen
Indiana

PEACH SAUCE.

BY MRS. CHAS. C. TOWNSEND.
(Wife of Representative from Pennsylvania.)

TAKE ripe, yellow peaches (clings preferred), pare and halve them. Throw in the kettle about two dozen of the peach seeds, and add one pint of boiling water to ten or twelve pounds of the fruit, and let it stew. After it has stewed down put in one-half pound of white sugar to every pound of fruit, and let stew down till it thickens. Seal up hot in jars.

Mrs. Charles. C. Townsend
Penna.

CHICKEN SALAD DRESSING.

BY MRS. H. C. M'CORMICK.
(Wife of Representative from Pennsylvania.)

TO the yolks of four hard-boiled eggs put through a very fine sieve, add the yolks of four raw eggs, a half teaspoonful of salt, and one-quarter teaspoon of cayenne pepper. Mix thoroughly in a wooden bowl, with a wooden spoon, adding gradually the clear juice of a lemon. When the mixture is as smooth as possible, add slowly, stirring constantly, one pint and a half of the best olive oil. If mustard is liked it is best to scald some, and add of that to suit the taste.

Ida H. M'Cormick
Williamsport
Pa.

CENTRAL AMERICAN SIRUP.

BY MRS. R. M. LA FOLLETTE.
(Wife of Representative from Wisconsin.)

FOUR pounds of sugar, almost white; one and a half pints of water; one teaspoon of pulverized alum. Put in a kettle and boil three minutes; strain while hot. For flavoring, three drops of essence of lemon to one-half gill of alcohol; add one teaspoonful of this to the above. This is a good substitute for honey.

Belle C. La Follette

MARYLAND EGG-NOGG.

BY MRS. STEPHEN J. FIELD.
(Wife of Associate Justice of the Supreme Court.)

ONE gallon of milk, one dozen eggs. Divide the yolks from the whites and beat them. Add fifteen tablespoonfuls of sugar, one grated nutmeg, one pint of brandy, one pint of Jamaica rum. Beat the yolks and sugar until light, add the brandy and rum, stirring constantly. Last of all put in one gallon of milk or cream and cover with the beaten whites of eggs.

REGENT PUNCH.

BY MRS. JOHN E. KENNA.
(Wife of Senator from West Virginia.)

ONE pound loaf sugar or rock candy, one large cup strong black tea (made), three wineglasses of brandy; three wineglasses of rum, one bottle imported champagne, two oranges (juice only), three lemons, one large lump of ice.

Annie B. Kenna.

MILK PUNCH.

BY MRS. ROSWELL P. FLOWER.
(Wife of Representative from New York.)

STEEP the thinly-pared rinds of eighteen lemons in one quart of proof whisky or rum (better) for three days in a closely-covered vegetable-dish. Then add five quarts of whisky, three quarts of boiling water, and pour it on the sugar and dissolve it; lemon juice (which has been squeezed and bottled when the lemons were peeled), white sugar three and a half pounds, grated nutmegs two; mix all in a large crock, and then pour in boiling milk two quarts. Let it stand till cool, stirring it well, then strain through a flannel bag as for jelly, the curds on no account to be removed until the liquor has been strained quite clear. Return the first quart to the bag, as it may not be quite clear, when strain through a flannel with filtering-paper. Bottle and cork well. It improves by age, and if properly prepared will keep all Winter.

Sarah M. Flower

APPLE TODDY.

BY MRS. JOS. E. WASHINGTON.
(Wife of Representative from Tennessee.)

BAKE twelve large apples till thoroughly done; put into a jar while hot and mash them well; pour on them three quarts boiling water; cover the jar and let stand till cool; then add three pints brandy, one pint Jamaica spirits, one-half pint of peach brandy, one-half pint curaçoa; sweeten to your taste. Let it stand a day or so, occasionally mashing the particles of apple; then strain for use. If apples are small use sixteen or eighteen. If you wish to keep the toddy add one pint brandy and more sugar.

Mary B. Washington

CIDER NOGG.

BY MRS. F. W. WHEELER,
(Wife of Representative from Michigan.)

BEAT to a foam the yolks of four eggs, with two tablespoons of pulverized sugar; add slowly two quarts of good cider. A little ginger may be added if desired.

Mrs. F. W. Wheeler

UNFERMENTED GRAPE JUICE.

BY MRS. ZERELDA G. WALLACE.
(Mother of Gen. Lew. Wallace.)

TAKE thoroughly ripe, fresh grapes, wash and take from the stem; put into preserving kettle as you would any other fruit, adding water enough to keep from burning. When thoroughly done, strain and boil; sweeten to suit taste; seal in bottles air tight. This is a refreshing drink for any one. Keep in dark, cool place of even temperature.

Z. G. Wallace

CABINET PUNCH.

BY MRS. JAS. B. RICKETTS.
(Widow of Maj.-Gen. Jas. B. Ricketts.)

POUR three quarts of boiling-water over three pounds of sugar. Add one pint of lemon juice, one pint of fine brandy or a quart of Jamaica rum. Mix well, and before using stir in one-half pint of peach brandy or cordial. This will make you a gallon and three-quarters of very nice punch.

FIG PUDDING.

BY MRS. BENJAMIN HARRISON.
(Wife of the President of the United States.)

ONE cup of black molasses, one cup of chopped suet, one cup of milk, three and a quarter cups of flour, two eggs, one teaspoonful of soda, one of cinnamon, half a teaspoonful of nutmeg, one pint of figs. Mix together the molasses, suet, spice and the figs, cut fine; dissolve the soda with a tablespoonful of hot water and mix with the milk; add to the other ingredients; beat the eggs light, and stir into the mixture; add the flour and beat thoroughly. Butter two small or one large brown-bread mold; turn the mixture into the mold and steam five hours. Serve with cream sauce.

Caroline Scott Harrison

MINCE PIES.

BY MRS. SAMUEL F. MILLER.
(Wife of Associate Justice of the United States.)

TWO pounds raw beef, chopped fine; two pounds suet, chopped fine; four pounds good tart apples, two pounds currants, two pounds raisins, two pounds citron, two pounds brown sugar, one quart good New Orleans molasses, four ounces of salt, one and one-half ounces mixed spices—cinnamon, cloves and allspice, with preponderance of cinnamon; one-half ounce white pepper, two nutmegs, juice of choice lemons, one quart brandy, one quart cider.

Mix dry parts with salt—that is, meat, suet and spices. Then put in apples, then fruit, then liquors, then sugar. Make two, and if possible six, weeks before using.

E. W. Miller

GRAHAM PUDDING.

BY MRS. W. H. H. MILLER.
(Wife of the Attorney-General of the United States.)

TWO and a half cups of graham flour, one cup of molasses, one cup of milk, one-half cup of melted butter, one egg, one cup of raisins, one teaspoon of soda, one teaspoon of cinnamon, one-half teaspoon of cloves, nutmeg to taste. Steam in mold three hours. Serve with pudding sauce of butter, sugar, etc. This is something like other plum pudding, with this difference—it is healthy.

Gertrude A. Miller

JELLY.

BY MRS. JERE. M. RUSK.
(Wife of the Secretary of Agriculture.)

TO one package of Cox's gelatine add one pint of cold water.. When dissolved, add one pint of hot water, two cups of sugar, juice of six lemons. Stir slowly until well dissolved, then strain into molds.

Elizabeth M Rusk.

TEMPERANCE PUNCH.

BY MRS. W. H. H. MILLER,
(Wife of the Attorney-General of the United States.)

ONE dozen lemons, one-half dozen oranges, prepared in the usual way; one pint of cranberries heated till the juice can all be easily extracted, and after cooling poured in with the lemon and oranges; water and sugar to taste.

Gertrude A. Miller

RUSSIAN CREAM.

BY MRS. JERE. M. RUSK.
(Wife of the Secretary of Agriculture.)

COVER one package of gelatine with cold water. When dissolved, add one cup of new milk, one cup of sugar; heat to boiling point, stirring frequently, then set away to cool. Whip one quart of thick cream until light, beat the whites of six eggs, and add both to the mixture; when cool, flavor with vanilla. Place the jelly in the bottom of the molds, and when stiff and cold add the cream; turn out of mold and serve in slices.

Elizabeth M. Rusk

FRUIT PUDDING.

BY MRS. PHILIP H. SHERIDAN.
(Widow of the General of the Armies of the United States.)

Fruit Pudding.

Line a mould with slices of sponge cake, then put in a layer of fruit, strawberries, raspberries, black berries, currants or ripe pineapple torn into bits— rich, tart, ripe fruit is best, pour over this a layer of hot custard, then another layer of cake & another of fruit and of custard until the mould is full, put away to get cold and firm and serve when turned out of the mould with sugar and cream. In the custard bring it boiling point in a farina kettle. To a pint of milk add an ounce and a half of dissolved gelatine, the yolks of four eggs and four ounces of sugar. When the custard has thickened be sure it doesn't curdle, take it off the fire and stir in a half pint of cream and the juice of a lemon.

Irene Rucker Sheridan

March 31st—
1890

CITRON PUDDING.

BY MRS. JOHN A. LOGAN.
(Widow of the late Senator from Illinois.)

ONE quart of fresh milk, one pint of stale bread crumbs (grated), four eggs, coffeecup of powdered sugar, less than one-half pound of citron (cut fine), juice and rind of one lemon, butter. Beat the yolks and sugar together; add by degrees the bread crumbs, milk and the rind of the lemon. Pour in a buttered dish; then drop in the citron and a piece of butter over all. Bake half an hour. When cold cover with the meringue made of the four whites, a cup of powdered sugar, the juice of the lemon; brown slightly and serve.

Mary S Logan

MERINGUE PUDDING.

BY MRS. M. C. BUTLER.
(Wife of Senator from South Carolina.)

FOUR level tablespoonfuls of corn starch, four eggs, four tablespoons of sugar, one and a half pints of milk. Make a custard of the eggs, sugar and milk; dissolve the corn starch in a portion of the milk and stir into the boiling mixture, stirring constantly to keep it smooth. Reserve the whites of two of the eggs; beat into a stiff froth, and after turning the pudding into a pudding-dish, spread the beaten whites, after sweetening, on the top, and set in the oven to brown. Flavor to suit the taste. Serve with cream.

Mrs. M. C. Butler

NEW ENGLAND INDIAN PUDDING.

BY MRS. HENRY W. BLAIR.
(Wife of Senator from New Hampshire.)

TWO quarts of milk, one cup of meal, one cup of molasses, half cup sugar, one teaspoonful of salt, one teaspoonful of cinnamon or ginger, two eggs. Heat one quart of the milk "milk warm," then slowly stir in the meal and keep stirring gently until it thickens but does not quite boil. Remove from the stove and add the molasses, sugar, salt and spice. Then beat the eggs well and stir them in. Pour into the pudding-dish, remove the mixing-spoon, and turn the second quart of milk in. Send immediately to the oven without mixing, and cook steadily five hours.

Eliza N Blair

SNOW PUDDING.

BY MRS. JAS. L. PUGH.
(Wife of Senator from Alabama.)

COVER one-half box of gelatine with cold water and let soak a half hour. Pour over it one pint of boiling water; add two cups of sugar, and stir until dissolved; add the juice of three lemons and strain the whole into a tin basin. Place this in a pan of ice-water and let it stand until cold. Then beat with an egg-beater until white as snow. Beat the whites of four eggs to a stiff froth, and stir them into the pudding. Turn the pudding into a mold that has been dipt into cold water, and set it away to harden. Make a sauce with the yolks of the eggs, one quart of milk, and a half-cup of sugar. Scald the milk; beat yolks and sugar together, until light, add them to the milk and cook two minutes. Take from the fire, add one teaspoonful vanilla, and turn out to cool.

Mrs. James L. Pugh

LOTTIE'S PUDDING.

BY MRS. WM. P. HEPBURN.
(Wife of the Solicitor of the Treasury.)

TWO and a half tablespoons of sugar, two tablespoons butter, three eggs, one tablespoon baking powder, three-fourths cup sweet milk, one cup chopped raisins, flour to make it the consistency of cake. Steam 45 minutes.

SAUCE.

One cup sugar, one-half cup butter, one cup rich cream, stirred together for half an hour, or until thoroughly mixed. Serve all cold.

M. A. Hepburn

RUSSIAN CREAM.

BY MRS. WM. S. HOLMAN.
(Wife of Representative from Indiana.)

ONE quart milk boiled, one-third of a box of gelatine dissolved in a small portion of the milk, six eggs beaten separately, the yolks beaten with a cup of sugar; then stir in gelatine and eggs into the rest of the milk, boil two minutes; pour over the beaten whites; pour into molds. Place on ice to cool.

Mrs A. K. Holman.

CREAM PIES.

BY MRS. C. A. BOUTELLE.
(Wife of Representative from Maine.)

MAKE the crust the same as for sponge cake, and bake in four deep tin pans. When cool split in two with a sharp knife and fill with the cream filling.

THE FILLING.

One pint of new milk, one cup of sugar, one-half cup of flour, two eggs, Put the basin of milk into another of hot water. Beat the sugar, flour and eggs together until very light and smooth, and when the milk boils stir in with one teaspoonful of salt. Cook twenty minutes, stirring often. Flavor with lemon, unless some other is preferred. This will fill the four pies. The pint of milk must be generous, and the half-cup of flour scant.

Mrs. C. A. Boutelle.

BOILED CUSTARD.

BY MRS. BYRON M. CUTCHEON.
(Wife of Representative from Michigan.)

TAKE one quart of new milk and bring it to a boiling heat in a double boiler. Add one teaspoonful of salt. Beat up four fresh eggs very light, and just before adding them to the milk beat in four heaping tablespoonfuls of sugar. Then take the milk off the fire and stir in the eggs and sugar slowly. Return to the fire and stir constantly until the custard begins to thicken. Then remove and strain through a fine wire strainer. Add vanilla or lemon or almond almond flavoring to taste. When the custard is cold beat in one cup of good rich milk.

PLUM PUDDING.

BY MRS. ELLIOTT B. COUES.
(Wife of the distinguished Scientist and Theosoph.)

THREE-QUARTERS of a pound of picked and finely-chopped suet; three-quarters of a pound of stoned raisins; three-quarters of a pound of well-washed and picked currants; one-quarter of a pound of candied orange peel and citron, cut in small slices; three-quarters of a pound of powdered sugar; three-quarters of a pound of bread crumbs; two peeled russet apples, cut in small slices; the grated peel of a lemon. Mix the whole thoroughly in a basin, with three pounded cloves, a pinch of salt, six eggs (one at a time), one-half gill of rum. Butter a pudding mold, fill it with the mixture, and tie a cloth over the top. Reverse a small baking sheet at the bottom of a stock-pot three parts full of boiling water. Put the pudding in it and boil for four hours, keeping the pot replenished with boiling water. Turn the pudding out of the mold on to a hot dish; sprinkle the dish with pounded sugar; pour in one-half pint of warm rum, and light it when putting the pudding on the table.

Mary Emily B. Coues

CHARLOTTE RUSSE.

BY MRS. ISAAC S. STRUBLE.
(Wife of Representative from Iowa.)

TAKE a sheet of very thin sponge cake and cut it in shape of a breakfast coffeecup; set this aside. Take a quart of double cream and whip it as though you whipped the white of eggs, as though you were making meringue; then add pulverized sugar, one leaf melted gelatine; flavor with vanilla; then pour into these cups while soft, and set it where it will stiffen.

Mrs I. S. Struble

CARDINAL RICHELIEU PUDDING.

BY MRS. CHAS. H. GIBSON.
(Wife of Representative from Maryland.)

TAKE eight eggs; beat whites and yolks separately; first balance the eight eggs with pulverized sugar and four eggs in flour, after it has been sifted twice; beat sugar and yolks together, then add the whites and the juice and rind of a large lemon; the rind must be grated fine. Last of all add flour, which must be cut in with a knife. Don't stir at all after adding flour. Grease a pretty mold (a Turk's head is the best) and pour the batter in. Bake quickly. Then make three pints of rich custard, the yolks of five eggs to a pint; sweeten and season with vanilla. When the cake is perfectly cold—it should always be made a day or so beforehand—cut it carefully across twice, and spread currant or pine apple jelly, or the preserved grated pine apple, between the layers of cake; put it together carefully so it will not be seen it has been cut; then have one-half pound of almonds blanched and stick them thick all over the cake with small, thin pieces of citron, and then pour one-pint of good sherry wine over the cake; let it stand all night; keep the custard on the ice, and just before dinner put the cake in a handsome dish and pour the custard all over it. This is a dish fit for the gods.

WOLF PUDDING.

BY MRS. R. H. NORTON.
(Wife of Representative from Missouri.)

ONE cup of brown sugar, one-half cup of butter, one cup of flour, one cup of blackberry jam, three tablespoonfuls of sour cream, one teaspoonful of soda, three eggs. This is to be mixed into batter. Serve with sauce.

*Mrs. R. H. Norton.
Troy Missouri.*

TAPIOCA CUSTARD PUDDING.

BY MRS. A. M. DOCKERY.
(Wife of Representative from Missouri.)

SOAK two tablespoons tapioca over night in cold water; when ready to make custard, boil one quart of milk; while boiling add beaten yolks of three eggs, three-fourths cup sugar, and the tapioca; turn it into the dish you wish to serve it in; have the beaten whites of the eggs ready, sweetened a little, and spread over the top; put it into the oven till a light brown. Eat cold.

Mrs. A M Dockery

CHARLOTTE RUSSE.

BY MRS. CHAS. S. BAKER.
(Wife of Representative from New York.)

ONE quart cream, one-half box Cox's gelatine thoroughly dissolved. Whip the cream to a froth, then sift in powdered sugar; strain the gelatine before adding; flavor and sweeten to taste. Line two molds or glass dishes; pour in the cream; set in the refrigerator to form.

Mrs Chas S Baker

SPONGE PUDDING.

BY MRS. W. E. MASON.
(Wife of Representative from Illinois.)

ONE pint milk, six eggs, two ounces flour, two ounces butter, two ounces sugar. Boil the milk, add the flour and then the sugar. When nearly cold add the butter. Separate the eggs, beat the yolks, and add the whites just before baking. Set pudding-dish into water to bake. Eat with sauce.

Edith J. W. Mason

BAKED CUSTARDS.

BY MRS. ALFRED C. HARMER.
(Wife of Representative from Pennsylvania.)

ONE pint of cream, four eggs, cinnamon, almond flavor, and three ounces of sugar. Boil the cream with a piece of cinnamon; pour it into a bowl, and when cold add the eggs well beaten and strained, the sugar powdered, and a few drops of almond flavor. Bake in small cups in slow oven.

Sarah E. Harmer.

CHARLOTTE RUSSE.

BY MRS. ALONZO NUTE.
(Wife of Representative from New Hampshire.)

MAKE a sponge cake in the proportion of three eggs and two-thirds of a cup of sugar. Bake it in a brick-shaped cakepan about four inches deep. Take one and a half pints of new cream; set it on ice till perfectly ice-cold; put one-fourth box of gelatine (more if the weather is warm) to soak in one-half cup of cold milk; whip the cream to a solid froth; fill up the cup of melted gelatine with boiling milk; let it get cold; put to the cream two cups of sugar, a tablespoonful of vanilla and a pinch of salt. Stir together the whipped cream, the gelatine and sugar, stirring constantly from the bottom, so that it will combine thoroughly without clotting before it is set. When the cake is done turn out on a sieve to cool. When cold place it bottom up in a clean pan the same size and shape of the first. Slice it crossways, taking out every alternate slice, without leaving a single crumb; then fill the spaces thus left with the mixture, filling in with a spoon carefully, a little in the bottom of each, holding the slices straight, till there is enough to keep them from tilting sideways. Fill up to the top and set on ice about six hours if the weather is hot. Serve in slices. Another pan may be filled with the odd slices.

Mrs A Nute

A PUDDING SAUCE.

BY MRS. JOHN B. HENDERSON.
(Wife of ex-Senator from Missouri

BRING a pint of milk to the boiling-point, and then stir in a generous teaspoonful of corn starch, previously rubbed smooth with a little of the cold milk; add also a tablespoonful of sugar. Let it cook for two or three minutes to thoroughly cook the starch, and then let the mixture get entirely cold. Flavor it with sherry or any of the flavorings, and just before serving stir in smoothly the whites of two eggs beaten to a stiff froth. As the egg froth is not cooked, the sauce will not keep very long at its best, perhaps half an hour.

Mary F. Henderson

APPLE PAN DOWDY.

BY MRS. MARCUS A. SMITH.
(Wife of the Delegate from Arizona.)

FOR a family of six, use two-quart pan. Pare and slice some good pie apples; place a layer of apples about an inch thick; season with sugar and a speck of salt. Put a layer of cracker crumbs half an inch thick; alternate apples and cracker till the pan is full. Bake one hour, and serve with cream or rich milk. Rhode Island greenings are best.

Elizabeth M. Smith

BOILED PEARS.

BY MRS. WM. H. MORROW.
(Wife of Representative from California.)

IN California, where fruits abound, nothing is more delicious than the pears. Take hard pears, remove rind and specks; be sure they are sound at the core; put into a fruit-kettle and cover with water; boil slowly one hour, then add a sufficient quantity of sugar to make a lively sirup; boil half or three-quarters of an hour longer. Serve cold.

Margaret H. Morrow.

APPLE TAPIOCA.

BY MRS. JOHN H. BANKHEAD.
(Wife of Representative from Alabama.)

ONE-HALF pound tapioca soaked over night in cold water. Make a quarter of a peck of apples into nice, rich, sweet sauce. Put the soaked tapioca in the sauce and let cook slowly until the tapioca is dissolved. Flavor with lemon or orange peel; sweeten to taste. Serve with cream sauce.

Mrs J. H. Bankhead
Birmingham
Ala.

PLUM PUDDING.

BY MRS. JOS. E. M'DONALD.
(Wife of ex-Senator from Indiana.)

THIS pudding is best when prepared, all but milk and eggs, the day before using. Seed and cut in half one pound of the best bloom raisins; pick, wash and dry before the fire one pound of Zante currants, commonly called plums; dredge the fruit well with flour, to prevent its sinking or clogging; take one pound of fresh beef suet, freed from the skin and string, and chop very fine; one pint of grated bread crumbs and a half pint of sifted flour; a large quarter of a pound of best sugar, a large tablespoonful of powdered mace and cinnamon mixed, and two powdered nutmegs; all the spice to be steeped in a half pint of mixed wine and brandy; put away these ingredients separately, closely covered, and let them stand all night. Next morning finish the pudding, which requires at least six hours' boiling. Beat wine and eggs together until very thick and smooth; then add one pint of rich milk, then the bread crumbs and flour; mix with the sugar the grated yellow rind and juice of two lemons, and add to the mixture gradually all the prepared ingredients, stirring hard. If too thick add more milk; if too thin add more bread crumbs; take care not to have too much bread or flour, or the pudding will be heavy; add two teaspoonfuls of baking powder, one quarter of a pound of citron; boil in tin molds; serve with lemon sauce, or with butter and sugar beaten to a cream and flavored with nutmeg and rose.

Josephine E. McDonald

CIDER JELLY.

BY MRS. D. J. BREWER.
(Wife of Associate Justice of Supreme Court.)

TAKE one package of Cox's gelatine; dissolve it in one pint of cold water. When it is thoroughly dissolved add one pint of cider and one quart of boiling water, (the cider must be sweet, and the very best;) to this add, also, two pounds of best granulated sugar, a pinch of ground cinnamon, the juice of two lemons, and the grated peel of one. Let it come to the boiling-point, strain and turn into molds. It must be kept in a cool place of course.

This is not only an excellent dish in a general way, being as good as wine jelly and clear as amber, but it is unequaled in sickness where stimulants are prohibited.

In warm weather it takes a little more gelatine to the same amount of fluid, than in cold weather.

Mrs. D. J. Brewer

DIXIE PUDDING.

BY MRS. W. H. F. LEE.
(Wife of Representative from Virginia.)

ONE pint of bread crumbs, one quart of milk, yolks of four eggs, rind of one lemon, one cup of sugar. Bake in pudding-dish. When done spread over with some kind of jams; beat the whites of the eggs light, season with the juice of lemon; one cup of sugar; put on top of pudding; set in oven for a minute to brown.

Mrs W. H. F. Lee

BREAD TOTÉ.

BY MRS. JOHN LIND.
(Wife of Representative from Minnesota.)

TWO cups bread crumbs, sifted and evenly browned or roasted, eight eggs (yolks), one and a half cups of granulated sugar, one-half pound chocolate (grated), three-fourths pound almonds, one-half pound citron, one-half teaspoon cinnamon, one-half cloves, one-fourth teaspoon cardamon, one-fourth cup brandy, juice and grated rind of one lemon. Mix sugar and yolks until very light; then add all ingredients except bread crumbs and whites of eggs, and stir well; then wet or dampen the crumbs with white wine and add to the rest last whites of the eggs well beaten. For icing, chocolate or a white frosting. Bake one and a half hours slowly.

Alice A. Lind
New Ulm
Minnesota

PUMPKIN PIE.

BY MRS. J. W. VAN SCHAICK.
(Wife of Representative from Wisconsin.)

THREE tablepoons of butter, two cups of sugar beaten together, three eggs, three cups of stewed pumpkin, one cup of cream, one wine-glass of sherry; also of brandy, nutmeg, cinnamon, and a little mace and salt to taste. Bake in a puff-paste.

PIE CRUST.

BY MRS. J. W. VAN SCHAICK.
(Wife of Representative from Wisconsin.)

TWO cups of flour, three-fourths cup of lard, one-half cup of butter, a pinch of salt; mix with ice-cold water—using a knife instead of the hand—into a firm dough. Roll it in a napkin and lay it on ice till the filling is ready; roll very thin, spread with butter and dredge with flour, repeating the process three times. Prepare the pie, and bake in quick oven.

Mrs. J. W. Van Schaick

SPANISH CREAM.

BY MRS. C. W. SPOFFORD.
(Wife of Proprietor of Riggs House, Washington, D. C.)

ONE quart of milk, four eggs, one-half box gelatine, one-half cup sugar; flavor with vanilla. Add gelatine to milk; boil slowly until dissolved; then add the yolks of the eggs and sugar beaten together. Cook like soft custard in a double boiler. Beat the whites of the eggs very lightly, and stir in lightly after taking from the stove; then set in molds. To be eaten with cream.

OLD-FASHIONED SPONGE CAKE.

BY MRS. M. R. WAITE.
(Widow of Chief Justice of the United States.)

TEN eggs (very fresh), one-half pound flour, one pound sugar (fine granulated), the grated rind and juice of a lemon, one saltspoonful of salt. Weigh the sugar and put it in the mixing-bowl; break the eggs, putting the yolks with the sugar and the whites in another dish. Beat the whites of the eggs until they will not drop from the rods; beat the yolks and sugar to a cream and until the sugar dissolves; strain the lemon juice and add it with the grated; put to the eggs and sugar. When the yolks and sugar are very light add the whites, beating all very hard until well mixed; sift the flour two or three times with the salt in it. If "New Process flour," take out one tablespoonful of it, as it takes less than the other kind. Add the flour a little at a time, stirring it in lightly. If the flour is beaten in, the cake will be tough. Put the mixture about one and a half inches thick into flat pans; sift fine sugar thinly over the top, and bake in an oven that is hottest at the bottom; try with a straw in about a half hour. If done it will not stick to the straw. Do not be alarmed if it falls a little when taken from the oven, but do not jar it or turn it out until it is partially cool.

Sincerely yours,
Amelia C. Waite.

GERMAN ALMOND RINGS.

BY MRS. WM. WINDOM.
(Wife of Secretary of the Treasury.)

ONE-HALF pound blanched almonds, one-half pound pulverized sugar, one-half pound puff-paste, whites of six eggs. Roll the paste very thin and cut out with a tumbler or tin biscuit-cutter. From each cut a smaller one from the center so that the ring will be three-fourths of an inch wide. Beat the whites to a stiff froth; then add the sugar and stir with the dish in boiling water until the meringue is quite thick. Into this stir the almonds, which have been previously sliced very thin. Cool. Then with a small silver knife place this mixture on the rings. Bake in an oven at the temperature proper for cake. Can be kept for two or three weeks.

Ellen T. Windom

SHAKSPERE CAKE.

BY MRS. WM. WINDOM.
(Wife of Secretary of the Treasury.)

ONE coffeecup of sugar creamed with one-half cup of butter; add three beaten eggs and beat thoroughly; add two cups of flour, into which one teaspoonful of cream tartar has been mixed, and at the same time, without stirring in the flour, three-fourths cup of milk into which one-half teaspoon of soda has been dissolved. Mix well. Lastly, add one-half pound English walnuts which have been cut fine. Bake in sheets a cake which shall be an inch thick when done. When partly cool frost with an icing made with the white of one egg and one cup of pulverized sugar, beaten ten minutes, and adding the juice of half a small lemon. When the icing has begun to harden a little, mark it in squares with the back of a silver knife, and lay in each square half of an English walnut.

Ellen T. Windom

ANGELS'-FOOD CAKE.

BY MRS. JERE. M. RUSK.
(Wife of the Secretary of Agriculture.)

TAKE whites of twelve eggs, one and a half cups pulverized sugar sifted three times, one cup flour, one teaspoonful of cream tartar. Sift flour and cream tartar together three times. Mix well with the sugar and stir into the beaten whites. One teaspoonful of flavoring.

Elizabeth M Rusk

HARRISON FRUIT CAKE.

BY MRS. JOHN J. INGALLS.
(Wife of Senator from Kansas, and President *pro tem.* of the Senate.)

ONE pound of butter, one pound of flour, one-quarter of a pound of sugar (fine granulated), one dozen eggs, two pounds of citron, two small cocoanuts (grated), two pounds blanched almonds, one wineglassful of wine, one wineglassful of brandy, one teaspoonful of ground cinnamon, one grated nutmeg, one teaspoonful of ground mace, two teaspoonfuls of baking powder, cream, butter and sugar and eggs, thoroughly beaten, but not separated. Mix baking powder with flour; then add, and lastly throw in fruit thoroughly chopped and floured. Bake in a slow oven. When done the cake will leave the sides of the pan.

Very Cordially Yours

A. L. C. Ingalls

DELICATE CAKE.

BY MRS. JOHN SHERMAN.
(Wife of Senator from Ohio.)

ONE pound of sugar (light weight), one pound of flour (light weight), a little more than half a pound of butter, whites of sixteen eggs beaten to a stiff froth; beat butter and sugar to a cream and add the flour and eggs alternately until all are used; flavor with peach or lemon. Bake in a moderately quick oven. No baking powder.

C. S. Sherman

BERWICK SPONGE CAKE.

BY MRS. WM. P. FRYE.
(Wife of Senator from Maine.)

SIX eggs, beat two minutes; three cups of sugar, beat five minutes; two cups of flour, beat one minute; one cup of cold water, beat one minute; two more cups flour, two teaspoonfuls cream tartar in the flour, beat one minute; one teaspoonful of soda put in the water, one teaspoonful of lemon and salt. Make in ten minutes, if everything is in readiness.

*Yours Sincerely,
Caroline F. Frye*

GINGERBREAD.

BY MRS. WM. P. FRYE.
(Wife of Senator from Maine.)

THREE eggs, one cup of molasses, one cup of sour milk, one cup of chopped raisins, one teaspoonful of soda (heaping), two cups of flour, spice to taste.

*Yours Sincerely,
Caroline Frye*

SPONGE CAKE.

BY MRS. JOHN H. REAGAN.
(Wife of Senator from Texas.)

TAKE the whites of twenty eggs, two gobletfuls of flour, three of pulverized sugar, two teaspoonfuls of extract of lemon essence, and one of cream of tartar. Sift the flour carefully, mix the sugar, eggs and lemon thoroughly and stir in the flour gradually, taking care not to toughen it by too much beating. The great test is in the baking. The oven should be very hot, and it should be baked but a few minutes, until it is a light brown.

Mrs. John H. Reagan,

SPONGE CAKE.

BY MRS. GILBERT A. PIERCE.
(Wife of Senator from North Dakota.)

ONE pound of sugar, one of flour, ten eggs. Stir yolks of eggs and sugar till perfectly light. Beat whites of eggs, and add them with flour after beating togething lightly. Flavor with lemon. Three teaspoonfuls of baking powder will add to its lightness. Bake in a moderate oven.

Mrs G. A. Pierce

SUNSHINE CAKE.

BY MRS. GIDEON C. MOODY.
(Wife of Senator from South Dakota.)

MAKE the same as angel cake, using one teaspoonful of orange extract instead of vanilla, and adding the well-beaten yolks of six eggs to the beaten whites and sugar before adding the flour.

Helen E. Moody.

MRS. CARLISLE'S CAKE.

BY MRS. JOHN G. CARLISLE.
(Wife of Representative from Kentucky, and ex-Speaker.)

THREE-FOURTHS pound of butter washed and creamed; add one pound of sugar, nine eggs beaten separately; add the yellows to butter and sugar, then one pound of flour and whites well frothed, added alternately; beat well and add two tablespoonfuls of baking powder just before baking.

Mrs. J. G. Carlisle.

WHAT-IS-LEFT-OVER CAKE.

BY MRS. JOHN H. GEAR.
(Wife of Representative from Iowa.)

IN making the cakes above, there may be small portions of the batter from each left. In such a case I have used it as follows, making a new cake, for which the above title is as good as any. Bake in layers and put together as follows: First a layer of fruit cake, then a layer of silver cake, another layer of fruit cake, then a layer of gold cake, a third layer of fruit cake, and last of all a layer of the snow cake. Spread jelly between; quince preferred. Cover with icing.

BREAKFAST CAKE.

BY MRS. NELSON DINGLEY, JR.
(Wife of Representative from Maine.)

ONE egg, one and one-half cups of milk, three cups of flour, one-half cup sugar, one teaspoon of soda, two of cream of tartar, a little salt and a tablespoonful of butter.

Mrs. N. Dingley Jr.

SPICE CAKE.

BY MRS. C. A. BOUTELLE.
(Wife of Representative from Maine.)

ONE-HALF cupful each of molasses, milk, sugar, butter, raisins or currants, two and a half cups of sifted flour, one egg, one-half teaspoon of cloves, one of cinnamon, one-half a teaspoon of soda. Beat the egg, sugar and butter together; add the molasses and the milk, in which should be dissolved the soda; then add the flour and spices and finally the fruit. Bake half an hour in shallow pans in a moderate oven. This is a good cake without fruit. Two sheets can be made with the quantities named.

STRAWBERRY SHORTCAKE.

BY MRS. JOHN M. FARQUHAR.
(Wife of Representative from New York.)

ONE quart of flour, three heaping teaspoons of baking powder; sift together thoroughly and rub in one ounce of butter; mix with a pint of sweet milk, using a spoon. The mixture will be softer than common piecrust. Do not try to mold or roll out the dough, but spread it on tins by patting with the hand till it is about an inch in thickness. Bake slowly till the cakes have had time to rise, then increase the heat. Split the cakes hot from the oven, spread the halves liberally with good butter, and cover them with fruit previously sweetened; place one on the other, the upper half reversed of course. Serve at once. When strawberries are gone, red raspberries or white currants are good in their place, and also peaches of a fine flavor. All these fruits should be sweetened an hour or two beforehand.

Mrs. J. M. Farquhar,

CARAMEL CAKE.

BY MRS. W. D. BYNUM.
(Wife of Representative from Indiana.)

THREE cups of sugar (sifted), one and one-half cups of butter, one cup of milk, four and a half cups of flour, five eggs well beaten, one small teaspoon of soda, two small teaspoons of cream tartar; mix and bake as jelly cake. For the filling, take three cups of burned sugar, one-half cup of milk, one teaspoon of butter, one tablespoon of browned flour, two tablespoons of cold water. Boil this mixture five minutes, then add three tablespoons of sweet almonds, roasted and ground to a powder; boil until it is the consistency of rich custard; add a pinch of soda, stir well, and remove from the fire. When cold spread between the layers of cake. Ice with almond icing.

Mrs. W. D. Bynum.

SPONGE CAKE.

BY MRS. LEWIS E. PAYSON.
(Wife of Representative from Illinois.)

SIX eggs, one-half pound sugar, one-fourth pound flour, juice and grated peel of half a lemon; rub the yolks of eggs and sugar to a cream; add lemon, then add the whites, well beaten; stir ten minutes; add flour the last thing and stir lightly. Bake in quick oven.

Mrs. Louise E. Payson

MINNEHAHA CAKE.

BY MRS. WM. P. HEPBURN.
(Wife of the Solicitor of the Treasury.)

ONE and a half cups of granulated sugar, half cup butter, stirred to a cream; whites of six eggs, two cups flour, one teaspoon and a half baking powder, half cup sweet milk. Bake in layers.

FILLING.

One cup of sugar, three tablespoons water, boiled candy high, poured over a cup of finely-chopped raisins (or hickory nuts), mixed with the well-beaten whites of two eggs; put between the layers of cake.

M. A. Hepburn

GOLD AND SILVER CAKES.

BY MRS. S. R. PETERS.
(Wife of Representative from Kansas.)

GOLD CAKE.

TWO cups of flour, three-fourths of a cup of butter, one cup of sugar, one egg and the yolks of eight eggs, two teaspoonfuls of baking powder. Make and bake in the usual way. Flavor to suit. The whites of the eight eggs can be used in Silver Cake.

SILVER CAKE.

Two and a half cups of flour, one-half cup of butter, two cups of white sugar, three-fourths cup of sweet milk, whites of eight eggs, two teaspoons of baking powder. Mixed and baked in the usual way, with any preferred flavoring.

Mrs S. R. Peters.

ENGLISH WALNUT CAKE.

BY MRS. W. H. GEST.
(Wife of Representative from Illinois.)

TWO cups of sugar, one-half cup of butter, one and one-half cup of milk, three cups of flour, four eggs, two teaspoons baking powder.

ICING.

Beat whites of two eggs, two cups powdered sugar, two teaspoons of chocolate. Spread between layers. Take one-half pound English walnut meats and arrange on top layer.

SPONGE CAKE.

BY MRS. JOSEPH M'KENNA.
(Wife of Representative from California.)

ONE pound granulated sugar, ten eggs. Beat eggs and sugar until very light; then stir in three-fourths pound of flour. Flavor with lemon. Bake one hour.

Amanda McKenna

GRANDMOTHER'S CAKE.

BY MRS. CHAS. A. RUSSELL.
(Wife of Representative from Massachusetts.)

ONE cup each of milk and butter, two of sugar, three of flour, four eggs, two even teaspoonfuls of baking powder, vanilla flavor; cream butter and sugar together; stir in the yolks of the eggs, add milk, sift flour and powder together and stir it into the mixture; add whites of eggs well beaten, and flavoring.

Ella S. Russell.

SNOW CAKE.

BY MRS. M. H. M'CORD.
(Wife of Representative from Wisconsin.)

WHITES of eight eggs, two cups of white sugar, one cup of butter, well washed; one cup of sweet milk, one teaspoon of soda and two of cream tartar sifted into two cups of flour, and one of corn starch. Beat the butter to a cream, then beat in the flour; beat the whites of eggs to a stiff froth, and beat the sugar into that; into this stir the milk, then add the two mixtures together. This can be baked in a loaf, but is better baked in layers, between which is spread a layer of boiled frosting, with almonds pounded to a paste, mixed into it; or with a spread of whipped cream between the layers.

FRUIT CAKE.

BY MRS. R. A. PIERCE.
(Wife of Representative from Tennessee.)

TWELVE eggs, whites and yolks beaten separately; one pound of white sugar and a cup of the best molasses; one pound of flour, browned; one pound of butter; one cup of sweet milk or cream, one heaping teaspoon of baking powder; one wineglass of brandy; one pound of citron, sliced very thin; one pound of raisins, stoned; two pounds of currants, well washed and dried; one teaspoon each of ground cloves, allspice and mace. Roll the raisins in the flour; mix all together, except the citron; put in a layer of the batter, then of the citron alternately till the pan is full. Bake in a moderate oven four hours.

CHOCOLATE CARAMEL CAKE.

BY MRS. J. W. FOSTER.
(Wife of ex-Minister to Mexico, Russia and Spain.)

FOUR eggs, two cups of sugar, one-half cup of butter, three teaspoonfuls of baking powder in cup of flour, one-half cup of milk and two more cups of flour.

CUSTARD TO PUT BETWEEN LAYERS.

Two-thirds pint of sweet milk or cream; raise to a boil, after which mix together four tablespoonfuls of sugar, one tablespoonful of corn starch dissolved in milk, the yolk of one egg well-beaten, and when done add the well-beaten white. Flavor with vanilla, and when cold spread between layers. This makes four layers, in two of which should be put grated chocolate to make them brown.

FROSTING.

One coffeecup of brown sugar, one-half cup of sweet milk, butter size of an egg, one tablespoonful of vanilla, one cake of Baker's chocolate. Mix together and boil slowly until it thickens; try like taffy, but do not make it too hard. Spread on the cake while hot.

Mary Parke Foster

COCOANUT CAKE.

BY MRS. R. H. NORTON.
(Wife of Representative from Missouri.)

TAKE two cups sugar, one-half cup butter, three cups flour, one cup sweet milk, whites of five eggs, four teaspoonfuls baking powder. Bake in five layers.

ICING.

Whites of three eggs, one-half a cup of sugar. Spread on the layers, and sprinkle thickly with ground cocoanut.

Mrs. R. H. Norton.
Troy
Missouri.

DELICATE CAKE.

BY MRS. H. C. M'CORMICK.
(Wife of Representative from Pennsylvania.)

THREE-FOURTHS cup of butter, two cups fine granulated sugar, beaten well together; one cup of sweet milk, three cups flour, two teaspoonfuls of baking powder and the whites of eight eggs. Flavor with almond. Beat well ten minutes after putting in all the ingredients. For loaf bake one hour.

Ida H. McCormick,
Williamsport,
Pa.

ICE-CREAM CAKE.

BY MRS. R. F. PETTIGREW.
(Wife of Representative from South Dakota.)

ONE cup of sugar, one-half cup butter, one-half cup corn starch, one-half cup milk, one teaspoon baking powder, whites of four eggs.

FILLING.

Two cups sugar, one-fourth cup water, or two tablespoons of water; boil until it hairs or will harden in cold water. Pour this mixture into the whites of four eggs well beaten. Chopped nuts improve the filling.

Mrs. R. F. Pettigrew

DROP CAKE.

BY MRS. ALONZO NUTE.
(Wife of Representative from New Hampshire.)

THREE eggs, two teacups of sugar, one coffee-cup of rich sour cream, (if not possible to get it rich, put two tablespoons of butter to it,) one-fourth a teaspoon of soda, one-half a teaspoon of salt, one-half a medium-sized nutmeg. Stir in slowly sufficient flour to make a thick batter, but not stiff—about the consistency of pound cake. Bake in muffin-pans, heated and well-buttered, dropping a tablespoonful of the batter in each ring. Baked in an oven that is well-heated at first, and grows cooler as they bake. One-third of a teacup of currants mixed in is an improvement.

Mrs A Nute

SAUCISSONS DE CHOCOLAT.

BY MISS. BESSIE SNIDER.
(Daughter of Representative from Minnesota.)

TAKE two cakes of "German's sweet chocolate," put in a pan, and the pan in another larger one of hot water; leave on the stove until thoroughly melted, taking care that nothing whatever is put in the chocolate; then keeping it in the pan of hot water, take to the table and pour in honey until the chocolate is easily molded; mix in a cupful of blanched sweet almonds cut into pieces about the size of a pea, a pinch each of powdered cloves and cinnamon. Then mold with the hands into rolls about five inches long and an inch thick; wrap in tin foil cut previously into sheets of the right size. Put in the refrigerator to cool. The little sausages will keep for months, and in fact grow better with age, to my mind. To serve them, slice into thin slices, and put in a dainty little bonbon dish.

*Very Sincerely yours,
Bessie Snider*

PECAN CAKE.

BY MRS. J. R. M'KEE.
(Daughter of the President.)

ONE cup of butter, two and a half cups of flour, two cups of sugar, one-half cup of sweet milk, whites of eight eggs, two teaspoonfuls baking powder. Beat together butter and sugar, add a little of the beaten egg; then put in a cup of flour, then some milk, then again flour and milk; put all the milk in with the second cup of flour, then add the rest of the egg.

ICING TO FILL AND PUT OVER TOP.

Whites of six eggs beaten stiff with powdered sugar, one small can of grated pineapple, and two cups of pecans, chopped fine. The nuts should soak awhile in the pineapple before mixing them into the egg and sugar. Put whole pecan kernels over the top of the cake while the icing is still soft.

Yours cordially,
Mary Harrison McKee

POUND CAKE.

BY MISS MARY E. TURPIE.
(Daughter of Senator from Indiana.)

ONE pound flour, one of butter, one of sugar, nine eggs. Wash the butter and beat it and the flour together. Beat the egg yolks and sugar together. When well-beaten mix all together, add the whites of the eggs well-beaten, and one-half teaspoonful baking powder. Bake one hour and fifteen minutes.

Mary E. Turpie

SPONGE CAKE.

BY MRS. ISABELLA BEECHER HOOKER.
(The noted Advocate of Women's Rights.)

ONE pound sugar, one-half pound flour, ten eggs, one lemon, salt. Beat the whites and yolks of the eggs separately and till very light; then mix the sugar with the yolks thoroughly; then add the grated lemon peel and the juice, and a little salt; then add the flour, cutting it with a large knife, moving the mass as lightly as possible and avoid beating entirely.

Isabella Beecher Hooker
Hartford Conn

FRUIT CAKE.

BY MISS MARY E. TURPIE.
(Daughter of Senator from Indiana.)

ONE pound each of sugar, butter, flour, seeded raisins, currants and citron; one cup of molasses, one-half cup whisky, one cup sour cream, one-half teaspoonful soda, one tablespoonful each of cinnamon, cloves, allspice, grated nutmeg and mace; nine eggs. Brown the flour, and bake four hours.

Mary E. Turpie

ANGEL FOOD.

BY MISS MARY E. TURPIE.
(Daughter of Senator from Indiana.)

TAKE the whites of seventeen eggs; one pound pulverized sugar, one-half pound flour, three-quarters of an ounce cream of tartar. Sift the flour, sugar and cream of tartar together seven times. Beat whites of eggs stiff; then sift the flour slowly into the whites. Bake in new pan that has never been used. Do not butter the pan.

Mary E. Turpie

BOILED FROSTING.

BY MISS MARY E. TURPIE.
(Daughter of Senator from Indiana.)

ONE cup of granulated sugar, one tablespoonful cold water. Boil until it ropes. Then pour in the white of one egg beaten stiff. Stir constantly until it is perfectly smooth.

Mary E. Turpie

CHOCOLATE-CREAM CAKE.

BY MRS. LILLAH BRICKNER.
(Daughter of Representative from Wisconsin.)

ONE cup of sugar and half a cup of butter creamed together; two cups of flour and one and a half teaspoons of baking powder sifted together; stir into the butter and sugar one-half cup of milk; stir in the flour and flavor with vanilla; beat the whites of four eggs to a stiff froth, stir into the mixture, and bake in a well-buttered mold. For the icing, boil together one cup of powdered sugar and one-half cup of milk till it thickens when stirred, when it must be taken from the stove and stirred till white, and thick enough to spread nicely, being careful to spread before it becomes too thick. Flavor with vanilla, and spread all over the cake, and then cover it with a thick layer of melted chocolate.

Lillah Brickner

BONBONS.

BY MRS. SHELBY M. CULLOM.
(Wife of Senator from Illinois.)

MIX together with the whites of two eggs an equal quantity of cold water and enough confectioner's sugar to make a stiff dough. It will require about two pounds. To prepare fruits and nuts, take seeds out of dates and fill with the cream; blanch almonds and cover with cream. Candied cherries are very nice; take little balls of the cream, and put a cherry on each. English walnuts are used in the same way as cherries.

Julia Cullom

CHOCOLATE CREAMS.

BY MRS. SHELBY M. CULLOM.
(Wife of Senator from Illinois.)

GRATE a package of sweetened chocolate, add two tablespoonfuls of water, and set the bowl in a tin of water on the stove to melt. While melting, roll some of the cream (see page 204) into balls; dip these one at a time in the chocolate, lifting out with a fork. Put on a buttered dish to harden. Use any kind of flavoring desired in cream.

Julia Cullom

CANDIED SWEET POTATOES.

BY MRS. M. C. BUTLER.
(Wife of Senator from South Carolina.)

BOIL, skin and slice enough sweet potatoes to fill a pudding-dish. Put a layer of potatoes in the bottom, then sprinkle a light layer of sugar over them, with some bits of butter, and a very little sirup; then another layer of potatoes, and so on till the dish is full. Place it in the oven and bake a rich brown.

Mrs. M. C. Butler

FROZEN APRICOTS.

BY MRS. M. S. QUAY.
(Wife of Senator from Pennsylvania.)

ONE can of apricots, a generous pint of sugar, a quart of water, a pint of whipped cream measured after being whipped. Cut the apricots in small pieces, add the sugar and water, and freeze. When nearly frozen add the cream.

Agnes B Quay

ORANGES FILLED WITH JELLY.

BY MRS. J. N. HUSTON.
(Wife of the Treasurer of the United States.)

TAKE half a dozen oranges that are perfect; make a hole at the stem end about half an inch in diameter; take a teaspoon and remove the pulp, and then soak the oranges in cold water for an hour; then scrape with the spoon until they are smooth inside; rinse with cold water, and drain on a cloth and put them in ice-box. Prepare pink and clear orange jelly, with the juice of two lemons added. Fill half of them with the pink, the other half with clear jelly, and when they are set wipe clean and cut each orange in four quarters. Heap them in a pretty glass dish for the table.

Mrs J. N. Huston

CRYSTALLIZED FRUIT.

BY MRS. CHAS. E. HOOKER.
(Wife of Representative from Mississippi.)

MAKE a wine jelly according to the recipe found in a box of Cox's gelatine, always using sherry wine, on account of its color. Have ready a mold of any shape, according to fancy, in which to crystallize the fruit in layers, of which use any delicious variety. The first layer could be of a banana cut in thin slices, placed at the bottom of the mold. Then pour over it some of the jelly; then of oranges, sweet and juicy, about two, with the seeds extracted, and cut in small pieces; then pour more jelly over this, and so on until you may have five or six varieties of fruit. For this recipe candied figs and limes are delicious. Mix through the fruit about two dozen English walnuts, well-minced up. As the layers of fruit are placed in the mold sprinkle a little sugar over each. When the mold is full of jelly and fruit put its top on securely, and keep it surrounded and covered with ice. When the contents of the mold are hard enough to slice, slip them out carefully and place on fancy dish, serving with whipt cream, the same as for Charlotte Russe.

ICE CREAM WITHOUT EGGS.

BY MRS. WM. VANDEVER.
(Wife of Representative from California.)

ONE quart new milk; set in a vessel of hot water; when it comes to the boiling-point add two large tablespoonfuls of arrowroot smoothly mixed with cold milk and two teacups of sugar; stir till smooth and thick. When cold add one pint of rich cream and flavoring to suit taste; put in freezer and turn rapidly.

Mrs. Wm. Vandever
Ventura
California

CARAMEL ICE-CREAM.

BY MRS. H. C. HANSBROUGH.
(Wife of Representative from North Dakota.)

ONE pint of milk, one quart of cream, three eggs, two cups of granulated sugar, one cup of pulverized sugar, one-fourth cup of corn starch. Beat the eggs, corn starch, and one cup of the granulated sugar together; stir in the milk while boiling; let it boil fifteen minutes; then stir the other cup of granulated sugar in a smoking-hot spider; stir quickly till brown; add to the boiling custard, stirring quickly. Set away to cool; when cool add the cream, whipped, and the cup of pulverized sugar. Flavor to suit. Freeze.

Josephine E. Hansbrough

ORANGE PRESERVES.

BY MRS. CHAS. TRACEY.
(Wife of Representative from New York.)

TAKE five dozen moderately tart oranges—be sure they are not bitter, and cover them with cold water over night. Next morning turn the cold water off, and cover them with water as hot as can be borne by the hand; then take off the rind and as much of the white inter-lining as possible. Quarter half of them, and slice the other half, taking out all the seeds. Take the rind of three or four of them, remove the white, and cut in small pieces, and put them in with your fruit. Then for eight pounds of the fruit take seven of white sugar, and let the whole simmer on a slow fire, skimming frequently, till it comes to a boil, then boil twenty minutes.

Hermine Tracey.

DEVILED ALMONDS.

BY MRS. W. D. OWEN.
(Wife of Representative from Indiana.)

BLANCH one-half pound of sweet almonds and wipe them dry; then put into a frying-pan two ounces of butter; make it hot; add the almonds; fry them gently till of a good brown color; drain them on a hair sieve; strew cayenne pepper and salt over them and serve hot.

Mrs. W. D. Owen
Indiana

SALTED ALMONDS.

BY MRS. JOHN F. LACEY.
(Wife of Representative from Iowa.)

TO a cupful of blanched almonds add one tablespoonful of melted butter. Stir well. Let them stand an hour; then sprinkle with salt, allowing a tablespoonful for each cupful of nuts. Put the almonds into a moderate heated oven, stirring occasionally while they are turning to a delicate brown. In about fifteen minutes they should be crisp.

Martha N. Lacey

ORANGE FOOL.

BY MRS. DANIEL M. RANSDELL.
(Wife of United States Marshal of the District of Columbia.)

MIX the juice of three Seville oranges with three whole eggs well beaten; one-half pint of cream, and cinnamon, nutmeg and finely sifted sugar to taste. Set this over a slow fire and stir, *one way*, until it becomes of the consistency of melted butter. Serve ice-cold.

Mary C. Ransdell.

CHOW-CHOW.

BY MRS. JOHN SHERMAN.
(Wife of Senator from Ohio.)

ONE-HALF peck of onions, one-half peck medium-sized cucumbers, one-half peck cauliflower (or cabbage will do), one-half peck green tomatoes, one-half dozen red peppers. Chop all—*not too fine*—salt, mix, and scald in three pints of vinegar and three of water. When well scalded drain from the vinegar, and pour over the following mixture: Six pints of vinegar, two and a-half cups of brown sugar, three-quarters of a pound ground mustard, one ounce turmeric, one-half pint olive oil, three-quarters of a cup flour. Mix the mustard, flour, oil and turmeric together with one pint of cold vinegar, and stir into the six pints of vinegar while boiling, having previously added the sugar and all kinds of spices. Celery or celery seed is an improvement.

C. S. Sherman

PRESIDENT HARRISON'S CHRISTMAS DINNER.

BY MRS. BENJAMIN HARRISON
(Wife of the President.)

MENU.
Blue Point oysters, half shell.
SOUP.
Consomme Royal.
ENTREE.
Bouches a la Reine.
ROAST.
Turkey, cranberry jelly.
Potatoes Duchesse. Stewed celery.
Terrapin a la Maryland.
Lettuce salad, plain dressing.
SWEETS.
Mince pie. American plum pudding.
DESSERT.
Ice-cream. Tutti-frutti.
Lady-fingers. Maccaroons. Carlsbad wafers.
FRUITS.
Apples. Florida oranges. Bananas.
Grapes. Pears.
Black coffee.

Caroline Scott Harrison

WEDDING CAKE.

BY MRS. F. W. LANDER.
(Widow of Gen. F. W. Lander.)

AN excellent wedding cake or so-called fruit cake: One pound citron, cut in thin slices, one pound flour; one pound sugar, one pound butter, beaten together well; one dozen eggs broken into, and well-beaten with, sugar and butter; two pounds raisins carefully stoned, two pounds best dried currants well cleaned, one pound blanched almonds cut fine, one wineglass of brandy, one-half teaspoon each of mace, cinnamon, allspice and cloves (powdered). Bake in a confectioner's oven, and let him frost it elaborately or plainly. (All ingredients to be of the best.)

Mrs. Gen.ᵉ F. W. Lander

A PINK DINNER IN APARTMENTS.

BY MRS. WM. M. STEWART.
(Wife of Senator from Nevada.)

THERE is no reason why one occupying apartments in a hotel should not make a home there; and I, for one, try to have mine so. Our dinners are made attractive, the same as when we kept house, and entertained on a larger scale. To illustrate, I will give a description of a pink dinner.

The table was set as usual when company is invited, only that pink was the prevailing color. First a scarf of pink satin, under lace, was laid across the middle of the table, and on this was placed the central ornaments. In the very center was a pot of ferns, with broad pink satin ribbon twined in and out of the open-work edge, and some la France roses arranged among the green. At each end of the central scarf were baskets of pink bonbons. The menu cards were tied with knots of the pink satin ribbon, with the name of the hostess on one end and date of the dinner on the other, painted in gold letters. The cards of the guests were pink flower petals; the gentlemen's a long lily leaf, and the ladies' a rose leaf. At the end of the dinner each couple exchanged cards as souvenirs.

Mrs. W. M. Stewart

A GOOD BAKING POWDER.

BY MRS. MARY A. DENISON.
(Author of "That Husband of Mine.")

BETTER than all the yeast powders is this one, which has been in use for twenty-five years in a family that knows what good things are: One-half pound tartaric acid, one-half pound best baking soda, one quart of flour. Sift thoroughly six or seven times through a fine sieve. This is stronger than ordinary baking powder.

Mary A. Denison.

HEALING PLASTER.

BY MRS. ROSWELL P. FLOWER.
(Wife of Representative from New York.)

TAKE one pound of rosin, one ounce of mutton-tallow, one ounce of camphor gum, one ounce of beeswax, one-half ounce of gum myrrh, one-half ounce of British oil, one-half ounce of cedar oil, one-half ounce of linseed oil.

Sarah M. Flower

TO CLEAN KID GLOVES.

BY MRS. C. K. DAVIS.
(Wife of Senator from Minnesota.)

FIRST rub them thoroughly with flour or cracker crumbs, and then wash in refined gasoline as you would wash a pocket-handkerchief.

Mrs. C. K. Davis

www.ingramcontent.com/pod-product-compliance
Lightning Source LLC
Chambersburg PA
CBHW031825230426
43669CB00009B/1231